GHOSTHUNTING
OREGON

T0151976

AMERICA'S
HAUNTED ROAD TRIP

Titles in the *America's Haunted Road Trip* Series:

GHOSTHUNTING
OREGON

DONNA STEWART

CLERISY PRESS

Ghosthunting Oregon
First edition, second printing

COPYRIGHT © 2014 by Donna Stewart

ALL RIGHTS RESERVED. No portion of this book may be reproduced in any fashion, print, facsimile, or electronic, or by any method yet to be developed, without the express permission of the copyright holder.

For further information, contact the publisher at:

Clerisy Press
An imprint of AdventureKEEN
306 Greenup Street
Cincinnati, OH 41101
clerisypress.com

Cataloging-in-Publication Data is available from the Library of Congress.
ISBN-13 978-1-57860-549-1 (pbk.); ISBN 978-1-57860-550-7 (ebook)

Distributed by Publishers Group West
Printed in the United States of America

Editor: Michael O. Varhola
Cover Design: Scott McGrew

Front cover photo courtesy of HISE Studios. Back cover and interior photos by Donna Stewart with the following exceptions: page 12, 169, 173 Visitor7/Wikimedia Commons; pages 18, 29, 56, 67, 85, 90, 99, 104, 156, 193, 226 Laura Schier; page 70 Finetooth/Wikimedia Commons; page 93 Debbie Tegtmeier; page 105 Michael Cornelius/ Flickr/CC BY-SA 3.0; page 114 Little Mountain 5/Wikimedia Commons; page 118 Friends of Yaquina Lighthouses; pages 127 and 130 Demi/Wikimedia Commons; pages 131, 143, 162 Ian Poellet/Wikimedia Commons; page 132 James Wellington/Flickr/CC BY 2.0; pages 150, 175, 181 AnotherBeliever/Wikicommons; page 184 Bluedharma/ Wikicommons. Photos from Wikimedia Commons are used pursuant to license CC BY-SA 3.0.

TABLE OF CONTENTS

Eastern Oregon   183

Acknowledgments

I WOULD LIKE TO THANK my editor, Michael O. Varhola, for believing in me and this book. Without his friendship and guidance, I doubt it would have been possible. Also thanks to Laura Schier, whose in-person nudging kept me going even on days I doubted myself and my abilities. When it comes to the paranormal, Laura has always been a voice of reason and a natural leader of our paranormal research team, Paranormal Studies and Investigations (PSI) of Oregon. Her knowledge and natural ability with photography have proven priceless to our team and have helped us identify scenes that often are mistaken as being paranormal. She is my rock and has kept me focused throughout this project.

I would also like to thank all of the people I met on my own haunted road trips who took time from their days and nights to speak with me and share their experiences. And although I did not get to meet them, I would like to thank the McMenamin brothers, who have preserved and cared for many of Oregon's historic sites.

Thanks to my team members at PSI of Oregon—Rick Stewart (my partner in crime for more than 30 years), Laura Schier, Bill Brimer, Chris Stewart, Lisa Stewart, Alicia Nukusuk, and Kira Henderson—for always keeping it real and for being a part of my extended family.

Thanks to my great friend Sharon Kincaid, who has been with me long-distance for five years on PSI-FI Radio and in person on many investigations. Your knowledge of demonology has proven invaluable to me and my team. And thanks for tolerating my quirks and inability to answer my phone most of the time!

Thanks to my friends Debbie Tegtmeier and Laura Schier for being my field photographers when my original photographs fell victim to a computer crash. I could not have accomplished this without you.

Thank you to my family, who endured all-night writing sessions, the extensive use of K-Cups for the Keurig, my thinking aloud, and occasionally my answering my own questions. These include my children, Chris, Danielle, and Matt, who always inspire me to push myself in directions that I never thought possible, and who understand my moods and never love me any less for them; my grandchildren, Annabelle, Brandon, and Ashton (and one yet to arrive)—you are everything to me, my heart and soul and everything in between, and who I love to the moon and back; and Rick, who knows me better than anyone in the world (and loves me in spite of that) and is always the lighthouse that guides me from the darkest storm.

Last but certainly not least, thank you to the three people who are no longer with me physically: my mom, Bobbie Harper; my dad, Stan Harper; and my "other mother," Betty Schier. Not a day goes by that I do not think of you or feel your presence around me. I believe with all my heart you are still here in some way, and it is for that reason I will continue to try to prove that the paranormal is not scary but just an extension of many beautiful lives. I love you and miss you. This book is for all of you.

Welcome to
America's
Haunted Road Trip

BY VIRTUE OF THE FACT you are reading this, there is a
pretty good chance that you believe in ghosts or are at least open
to the idea that something referred to as such might be real. If so,
you are in good company, as surveys over the years tend to show
that more than half of all Americans believe in ghosts and other
supernatural phenomena. In fact, some 61% of participants in a
September 2013 *Huffington Post* poll indicated that they "believe
some people have experienced ghosts." (This overall percentage
skew up by as much as 8% and down as much as 16% based on
factors like gender, age, political affiliation, race, education, and
geographical region.)

Paranormal phenomena you or those you know might have
experienced can vary widely, from the subtle to the profound
and the comforting to the disturbing. Many people not seeking supernatural experiences have felt the presence or touch of
recently departed loved ones, for example, or even seen them,
often just once, as if in final farewell. Others have at various
points, and perhaps in places reputed to be haunted, experienced things like disembodied footsteps, inexplicable cold spots,
or sounds with no discernible source, including someone calling their name.

Those who are psychically sensitive, exposed to extremely
haunted sites, or actively engage in paranormal investigations—
including what have been widely referred to for some years now

as ghost hunts—might experience any number of other things as well. These can include anomalies not audible to the naked ear or visible to the naked eye captured in recordings or photographs, such as electronic voice phenomena (EVPs), orbs, mists, or even coveted full-frontal apparitions.

Our intent with the *America's Haunted Road Trip* series is to provide readers with resources they can use to personally discover and explore publicly accessible places that might be haunted. We are not trying to prove that any particular place is or is not haunted—every single one of the places that appears in *Ghosthunting Oregon* certainly could be, and author Donna Stewart firmly believes that a number of them definitely are. Rather, the purpose of this volume is to inform everyone from the casual historical traveler to the hard-core ghost hunter about places of potential interest and to provide concrete information about how to visit those places.

All of the places covered in this book (and the other volumes of the *America's Haunted Road Trip* series) are, to a lesser or greater extent, publicly accessible. Therefore, the sorts of places we cover in our guidebooks include bridges, churches, and other places of worship; cemeteries and graveyards; colleges and universities; government buildings; historic sites; hotels; museums; neighborhoods and districts of towns or cities; parks; restaurants and bars; roads and highways; railroads; shopping areas and malls; sports stadiums; and theaters.

Cemeteries, somewhat counterintuitively, are dismissed by some paranormal researchers, who feel they are not particularly good venues for paranormal investigation, but I disagree, as does Donna, who includes several in this volume.

"There are those who say that cemeteries are not haunted," Donna told me. "And there are those who say that they are among the most haunted places in the world. There is really no evidence to prove either statement. But if, in fact, a ghost is comprised of energy and needs it to communicate, it stands to reason that cemeteries would be rife with hauntings. When we display emotion in any form, we emit very strong energy. When we are angry, it affects those around us, and the energy of anger can cause fear and uneasiness. When we are happy, it also affects those around us, and the energy will make others feel happy, smile, and laugh. And when we grieve, we are emitting a wide range of emotion, from sadness to anger to happy recollections. The energy of emotions remain, and perhaps supplies the needed boost for ghosts to manifest."

Donna also includes a significant number of theaters in *Ghosthunting Oregon* and explained her thoughts on this to me during one of the many discussions on paranormal investigation we have had over the years.

"There are many theories about why ghosts tend to remain in theaters, but I hold fast with my thoughts on theaters or any other building for that matter—history. History inspires emotion, and if you have ever seen a play, you can see the passion actors have for their roles, and they also invoke emotion from an audience. Emotion is a conductor for paranormal energy, so it would seem that older theaters are replete with reasons for paranormal activity to exist.

"Theaters are also full of superstitions, which can lead people to believe they are experiencing something paranormal or, according to some, even lead to manifestations of paranormal activity. There are even superstitions regarding ghosts that may haunt theaters. Even today some people believe theaters should be closed one night each week, traditionally Monday, to give the ghosts residing there a chance to perform.

"A specific ghost that is highly revered, and a fall guy at the same time, is Thespis, from whom the word *thespian* is derived, and he held a place of high regard and privilege in theaters of old. Many believe Thespis of ancient Athens was the first person to ever utter written lines as an actor on the stage, and some claim that any unexplainable mishap that may befall a theater group can be blamed on him—especially on November 23, which, according to tradition, was the date he spoke those first lines.

"Another superstition regarding ghosts is that a light should always be left burning in a theater after it has been locked up for the night. One reason is to ward off any ghosts that may be lingering there. Another is to provide light for ghosts to see because failure to do so may result in them becoming mischievous. Yet another reason is to allow theater personnel to cross the stage safely so that they do not fall and join the resident ghosts."

Haunted theaters could, in fact, form the basis for an entire book, so I am glad Donna decided to cover several of them here.

The sorts of places we do not cover in our guidebooks or encourage people to visit include elementary, middle, or high schools; assisted living facilities; private homes and residential apartment buildings; private property; or prohibited areas like abandoned mental hospitals or condemned buildings. It also bears mentioning that all potentially haunted places, their proximity to the otherworld notwithstanding, are still subject to all the hazards of the real world. So show due respect to other good people and watch out for bad ones, do not fall afoul of local laws, be prepared for environmental hazards, and in keeping with the mantra of outdoor exploration, "take nothing but photographs, leave nothing but footprints."

Beyond that, we hope this book and the others in the series will be useful to you and that you have an enjoyable, informative, and fulfilling journey on your own haunted road trip.

Michael O. Varhola
Editor, *America's Haunted Road Trip*
varhola@varhola.com

Introduction

I **WAS 6 YEARS OLD** when the paranormal found me. It was not something I was seeking at that age, but nonetheless, there it was.

My grandfather had just passed away, and family and friends were gathered at my grandmother's home after his funeral services. It was getting dark outside, but a freakishly large snowfall the week before made it uncommonly bright. As the guests ate and talked in the living room, a bright flash of pink and a loud boom came from inside the house. All conversation ceased and everyone could hear footsteps in the hall that seemed to be walking closer. Then the footsteps were in the same room, and finally they faded toward the back door.

My grandmother's guests, pale and shaking, did not stay long after this incident. I remained with my grandmother for the week after the services. No one told me that this was something of which I needed to be afraid. And I wasn't afraid, not then nor when I felt someone sit on the edge of my bed and I awoke to see my grandfather, nor when my grandmother and I let the dog out before bed one night and saw my grandfather standing in the backyard, smiling, the wind tossing his thick, black hair. At the age of 6, I had more of a comprehension of death than I would have liked, but he was my grandfather, dead or alive, and I was not afraid.

I can explain some of that now, such as the boom and the flash of pink. Thunder is not a stranger on the Oregon coast, and that could explain the boom. This was the only substantial snowfall—3 feet—I can recall in Oregon coast history, so many did not even consider that lightning could produce a pinkish hue when reflecting off of snow. These things I can explain today, but I cannot explain the footsteps. I cannot explain seeing my grandfather sitting next to me, and I cannot explain my grandmother and me seeing my grandfather in the backyard. These images are still vivid in my memory, and I can see them as clearly now as I write this as I did more than 40 years ago. I wasn't looking for the paranormal. It was looking for me.

The following year, at 7, my best friend died after going into the hospital for a tonsillectomy and having an allergic reaction to the anesthesia. Before I knew he was gone, I was in my bedroom playing when I heard a tap at the bedroom window. I stood on my bed and looked outside, and there stood my best friend, smiling and waving me out. "Come on! Let's go exploring!" I heard him say. So I hopped off my bed and ran into the living room to tell my mother that I was going outside to play with Danny. She looked confused and shocked, and then she slowly told me that Danny was gone. I thought she was joking and told her that he was right outside my window and wanted to play. She looked outside, and then came and took my hand and led me outside to show me that no one was there. It was my turn to be confused and shocked. My mom then explained to me why Danny was gone, and that he was not coming back. Again I wasn't looking for the paranormal; it came looking for me.

At that time no one used the word *ghost* except in relation to Halloween, and no one used the word *spirit* except in church. So I had no explanation for what I had seen and heard, not even a word for it. To me, it was just my grandpa and my best friend.

Years later, the paranormal found me again. I was 14 and loved recording my favorite songs from the radio onto a shoebox tape recorder. One night, very tired, I slipped a tape in, hit RECORD, and fell asleep. When I awoke the next morning, I played it to hear what songs I recorded and was baffled when I heard voices over the music. They were not the voices of the male disc jockeys but were female voices, whispering a word or two throughout the recording. I let my friends listen, and they couldn't explain it either. But this was the first time I heard the word *ghost*.

This was the 1970s, and I had no one to talk to about this kind of phenomena, the library had no books on the topic, and the term *electronic voice phenomena* (EVP) had not even been coined yet. I knew I could not be the only person in the world to record voices like this, but I couldn't find anyone else with similar experiences. My friends were scared, but I was curious. If I had encountered ghosts, I wanted to know how and why they spoke through recorders. I wanted to know why I could not see them. I wanted to know what heaven was like. Each day, the list of things I wanted to learn about the paranormal grew longer. Each day I would set up my tape recorder at random times and let it record. And each day I would walk around my apartment complex with my little 110 camera, snapping pictures at nothing and saving babysitting money to get them developed as quickly as possible. But I still had no one to talk with about it all.

More than two decades passed and reality television was born, including the reality-based show *Ghost Hunters*. This opened up the door for many paranormal researchers and made paranormal research more socially acceptable. While any reality show is scripted to an extent, it did provide some basic groundwork for investigations that those in field had been struggling with for a long time. On the downside, suddenly everyone and their neighbor wanted to be a ghost hunter, and our small field was overrun with people who thought it was cool to provoke and disrespect the spirits. Paranormal reality shows encouraged everything that respectable paranormal researchers were against and became another mess we had to fight through.

Today, as paranormal reality television is coming to an end, we are once again making progress. Many of the overzealous ghost hunters quit once they realized they were not going to become rich and famous, while those dedicated to the field, to finding answers and learning more, are still going strong in that direction.

If you do a Google search for paranormal equipment, you will come up with more than 6 million results in 0.3 second. You will find fancy gadgets with all the bells, lights, and whistles. The truth is, however, little equipment is made strictly for the paranormal field because we simply do not know what a ghost is. Back in the 1980s, on a show called *Unsolved Mysteries*, someone decided that a ghost emits an electromagnetic field, so EMF meters shot up in sales; there is no evidence that a ghost has anything to do with EMF, yet people started making money off a tool that was built for electricians. The EMF meters got a little fancier as time went by—the K-II meter, the Mel Meter, the Trifield Meter—all the new ghost hunters had to have them, and they used them without even knowing why. Then came the infrared thermometers because someone decided that ghosts cool the air as they manipulate energy to manifest. Again, there is no proof of this, but innumerable ghost hunters began packing these gun-shaped thermometers just like the mechanics and chefs they were created for did. Pretty soon, everyone was in on the action and making ghosthunting devices, including fancy infrared lights, UV lights, full-spectrum lights, laser grids, and the much-sought-after status symbol, the thermal imager. There is no proof that any of these help detect paranormal phenomena, but they sure do make some ghost hunters look and feel important.

This book and all the other books in the *America's Haunted Road Trip* series are travel guides filled with publicly accessible locations you can visit and test your own investigative skills if you wish. You do not need an arsenal of equipment to do this. When you speak with paranormal researchers who have been in the field for decades, you will find that most of them carry minimal equipment and use basic tools. I use an Olympus digital voice recorder, a Sony digital camera, and a pretty awesome flashlight. My team, PSI of Oregon, does have infrared cameras in our equipment case to monitor investigations, and we carry EMF meters for residential investigations to rule out EMF leaks in homes that could cause a number of relevant side effects, such as hallucinations and paranoia. But our best evidence—or data, as we prefer to call it—has been the product of three simple tools that nearly everyone has: a camera, a voice recorder, and a flashlight. If you are planning to visit any of the locations in this book, you will also find that taking such simple tools saves considerable luggage space. And the most important tool is one you carry with you at all times—your intuition.

All of the locations in this book are purportedly haunted, and it is a pleasure to share them with you. I am not, however, trying to convince anyone that any or all are rife with ghosts at every turn. I have witnessed many paranormal encounters, but my experiences span four decades and are not the norm. My hope is that you find the book interesting enough to visit a few of the locations and discover the paranormal for yourself. And if you do stumble across a ghost, I would love to hear about it. But most of all, I hope your adventure is as rich and entertaining for you as writing this book was for me.

Donna Stewart
Coos Bay, Oregon
July 2014
ghosthuntingoregon@gmail.com

Greater Portland Area

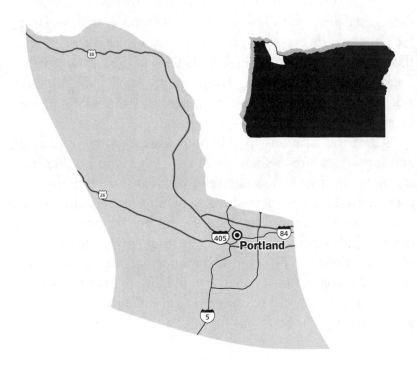

Portland
- Bagdad Theatre
- Benson Hotel
- Cathedral Park
- ComedySportz
- Heathman Hotel
- Hollywood Theatre
- Lone Fir Pioneer Cemetery
- Oaks Park
- Shanghai Tunnels
- Stark Street
- White Eagle Saloon
- Witch's Castle

CHAPTER 1

Bagdad Theatre
PORTLAND

ASIDE FROM ITS GHOSTS, the Bagdad Theatre has other claims to fame. In 1975, Hollywood came to the Bagdad Theatre when Jack Nicholson, Louise Fletcher, and Michael Douglas attended the Oregon premiere of the now-classic film *One
Flew Over the Cuckoo's Nest*. And in 1991 it hosted the Oregon
premiere of *My Own Private Idaho*, which starred River Phoenix
and Keanu Reeves, less than two years before the film world lost
Phoenix.

Universal Studios funded construction of the Bagdad Theatre in 1927 for $100,000, spending $25,000 of that on a state-of-the-art organ. It wasn't meant to be just another theater on a corner in the Hawthorne District of Portland but instead a centerpiece for an entire neighborhood and something to be admired. Taking up four city lots, the Bagdad rose five stories high and had the capacity to seat 1,500. In keeping with the "movie-star style" of Universal Studios, they held nothing back when it came to making the theater a sight to behold.

The Bagdad had no specific style but was a cross between Middle Eastern and Spanish styles and was proudly described as "an oasis of entertainment." Most theaters in the area at that time leaned toward a Middle Eastern theme, and the Bagdad also played to that, dressing its ushers in Arab-style attire.

People in the Hawthorne neighborhood in Portland waited on the edges of their seats for the January 14, 1927, grand opening, and it certainly did not disappoint. On hand was Portland mayor George Baker, who was himself a former theater owner, as well as silent film star Marilyn Mills. During the grand opening, the only lights to be seen in the neighborhood were those of the Bagdad marquee and the search lights that played across the night sky. Although the theater was able to seat 1,500 attendees, hundreds were left outside to celebrate in the bitter rain.

Because of its partnership with Universal Studios, the Bagdad was the only theater besides the larger downtown theaters that was allowed to show first-run films. It brought a small bit of Hollywood to the Hawthorne neighborhood. Even orchestra director Leon Strashun was a star in his own right, having studied with Peter Tchaikovsky and played lead violin at the Metropolitan Orchestra in New York.

Opening two years before the talkies debuted, the Bagdad also hosted live stage shows, live orchestra performances, and vaudeville acts. And when there were no acts scheduled, people were happy to simply wander the theater and admire the decor, the fountain, the murals, and the female ushers dressed as "Arabians." The Bagdad made its way into the hearts of many Portlandians.

The Bagdad changed successfully with the times, from silent films to talkies, always offering a wide variety of movies and entertainment. During the Prohibition era it is rumored that the theater included a speakeasy, and in the 1970s it was home to an art house and a hippie hangout. Everyone was welcome at the Bagdad.

Not long after the premiere of *One Flew Over the Cuckoo's Nest,* it became apparent that the Bagdad was in need of some cosmetic repair. At that time, brothers Mike and Brian McMenamin bought the theater, restored it, added a pub, and opened the doors once again to enthusiastic movie lovers as the Bagdad Movie House and Pub. They hosted the premiere of *My Own Private Idaho* and Michael Moore's *The Big One.*

The McMenamins are well known in the Portland area for buying and restoring old theaters, ballrooms, hotels, and pubs and turning them all into thriving businesses. Most of the locations they buy and restore have a strong haunted history. The Bagdad Theatre is no different—it has a long record of paranormal activity. People seem to know who the ghosts of the Bagdad are—at least most of them.

There is speculation that those who die in theaters, whether by suicide, murder, or accident, often remain there because of an emotional attachment to the site, because they loved to act, or because they enjoyed the job they held there. Maybe some of them just continue on with what they did in life or keep an eye on how others now perform their jobs.

One story claims that a former stagehand—a young man who wanted to be on the stage instead of behind it—committed suicide in the Bagdad's backstage area and can now often be seen crossing in front of the screen and heard whispering behind it. So perhaps in death, he has achieved his dream of being a performer.

Another ghost seems concerned about the work done by employees. Papers are often shifted, cleaning supplies are moved or removed from a room altogether, and many workers have reported hearing footsteps following them during the night as they performed their duties. This is especially common in the kitchen, the swinging doors to which are often seen moving with no explanation, as if someone were leaning against them on the other side.

"Nothing bad," one young woman told me. "It just feels like a mom or a grandma making sure I am doing it the right way. So I try to do it the right way."

A more discomforting type of ghost is often seen, heard, and felt in the downstairs restroom. Many claim to have heard someone walk in while they were in the restroom. They smelled men's cologne, and they had the strong feeling that someone was watching them from over the top of the stall. And while no one has claimed to feel threatened, they do say it is an awkward sensation. The last place anyone would want to feel spied on is in a bathroom stall.

"All that came to mind was that old men's cologne called Hai Karate; it was that tacky and pungent," one woman who said she had had a similar experience and heard footsteps in the restroom told me with a laugh. "Did I feel like I was being watched? Not really. I mean, I couldn't get over the bad cologne! And, seriously, if a dead guy wants to peek over a bathroom stall at me, all the more power to him. Who says ghosts can't be playful now and then?"

I agreed. And I loved her attitude toward ghosts and the paranormal.

Other random activities could be attributed to the paranormal but do not seem to be affiliated with any specific ghost. It could be that many spirits linger at the Bagdad.

People claim to have seen a young female sitting in different seats in the theater, for example, never making a noise and only visible for a few seconds before fading away. There have even been reports of children playing in the aisles. But when people notice and mention the sounds, they cease immediately.

One thing is for certain—the history of the Bagdad is alive within the restored walls. It is still quite the sight to behold in Portland.

The Bagdad is now a first-run theater with a screen that is 50% larger than in most theaters. It boasts a 20,000-watt surround-sound system, a K Prime digital projector, and lush rocker seating. Everything is state-of-the-art at the Bagdad, including closed captioning and other options for the hearing impaired.

Like the theater itself, the concession stand has grown up and into the 21st century as well. Tried-and-true treats like popcorn, sodas, and candy remain, but visitors can also enjoy an expanded menu that includes items like fresh-baked pizza, a selection of tap beers, and an ever-growing menu of delicacies. The theater also has gluten-free selections, vegetarian selections, and a host of burgers and sandwiches. And you don't need to wait in long lines because your food can be delivered right to your theater seat.

You will still get a grand glimpse of the Bagdad's heyday as soon as you enter the theater, with its balconies, vintage lighting and decor, and massively high ceilings. It is a combination of luxury and history that will not disappoint. Enjoy a movie in comfort, have a microbrew or two if you are so inclined, and meet the ghosts that might be seated right next to you.

CHAPTER 2

Benson Hotel
PORTLAND

WHILE MOST PURPORTEDLY HAUNTED locations in the Portland area are home to a single ghost or type of haunting, the Benson Hotel reportedly houses five spiritual apparitions, each similar in description and related activity.

Research on Simon Benson will find his name associated with numerous buildings and locations in the Portland area. Among them are a high school, the Benson Hotel, and 20 brass water fountains called Benson Bubblers throughout Portland's downtown district. Benson was, without argument, a Pacific Northwest success story.

One of seven children, Simon Berger Iverson was born in Gausdal, Norway, in 1852. He and his family immigrated to the United States in 1867 when he was 16 and, shortly after their arrival, they changed their name from Iverson to Benson and proceeded to become US citizens.

Benson's early career included work as both a farmhand and as a logger with a sawmill. When he was 24 he opened a general store in Wisconsin and operated it for three years until it was destroyed by a fire. At 27, with a wife, Esther, and son, Amos, to care for, Benson found himself in financial ruin.

The lure of the prospering timber industry in the Pacific Northwest, combined with his experience in sawmills, led to Benson packing up his family and moving to Portland in 1880. Settled in Portland, Simon and Esther added two daughters, Alice and Caroline, to their family. In 1891, Esther lost a lengthy battle with tuberculosis, and in 1894, Benson married Pamela Loomis and added two more sons, Gilbert and Chester, to his family.

Success was not immediate for Benson, nor was it without hard work and determination, and his family struggled through periods of poverty before he began buying up timber tracts when and where he could. He later built the Benson seagoing rafts, which were able to carry up to 6 million board feet of timber and drastically cut the cost of transporting logs to California. And in 1898, he moved his business headquarters to Portland.

In 1912, Benson felt the need to attract tourists to the Portland area that he loved so much. He began construction on a hotel that sat adjacent to the Oregon Hotel and, with this proximity in mind, tentatively named it the New Oregon Hotel. It became known around Portland as the Benson Hotel, however, and 16 months later, when Benson took over management of the establishment, he renamed it just that.

The Benson Hotel, with its 12 stories of red brick and cream-colored terracotta, was modeled after the Blackstone Hotel in Chicago. And the exterior was only the beginning of the Benson experience. The lobby of the Benson boasted rare Circassian walnut woodwork from Russia, Italian marble flooring, and massive chandeliers made from Austrian crystals. Simon Benson had created more than a luxury hotel—he had created a work of art.

Along with its visual allure, the Benson Hotel also offered the best in modern conveniences, including private baths, automatic door switches, electric lighting, and telephones in every room. The Benson Hotel did, and still does, attract an elegant clientele, and celebrities, politicians, and even US presidents have frequented it.

The Benson Hotel was thoroughly renovated and restored in 1991 and thrives today as it did in the early 1900s. It is, in fact, so beautiful and welcoming that some guests never leave.

People have reported numerous ghosts in the Benson Hotel, and many guests check in hoping to meet one of them face-to-face. While paranormal experiences have occurred throughout the hotel, the majority of the activity centers on the 7th, 9th, and 12th floors. Both guests and staff have experienced that activity.

The most well-known ghost is that of Simon Benson himself, and as much as he adored his hotel, it makes sense that it is where he would choose to spend his afterlife. Many have seen the image of Benson, attired in a formal period suit, slowly descending the staircase into the lobby. Others have seen him roaming about the common area of the hotel, often scowling at guests because—many believe—he does not like them partaking in alcohol in his beloved hotel. Often, when the scowl does not work, his ghost has been known to physically knock over a drink here and there.

One employee claims to have seen the ghost of Benson in the banquet area, although that time he had discarded his

formal attire for lumberjack clothing. The employee was setting the tables for a banquet when Benson entered the room and
then just as quickly exited into the wine storage area, vanish-
ing before her eyes. Shaken, she nervously finished her job as
quickly as possible, glancing over her shoulder to make sure she
was still alone in the room.

Other employees claim to have seen the ghost of Benson in
one of the meeting areas, standing quietly and attentively in the
back of the room as an important meeting commenced.

Another popular ghost at the Benson Hotel is that of a young
boy, around the age of 3 or 4, who witnesses describe as thin
and with short, light brown hair. Some local psychics have said
that it is the ghost of Jimi Hendrix Experience drummer John
Ronald "Mitch" Mitchell, who died at the Benson Hotel in 2008.
Mitchell was a famous child actor in England before embarking
on a career in rock and roll, and the psychics believe he remains
at the Benson as the child version of himself. While anything
may be possible in the afterlife, this does beg the question as
to why this young boy has been seen at the hotel for decades
whereas Mitchell died in 2008.

**Formerly the New Oregon Hotel, the century-old Benson Hotel stands tall
today.**

One guest who was in Portland on business checked into a room on the seventh floor of the Benson Hotel. She was in bed and growing weary of the movie on television, so she turned off the set and checked her cell phone one last time for any messages from her family before turning in. Then, when she rolled over, she came face-to-face with a little boy who stood at the side of her bed. She estimated the child to be about 3 years old, and as a mother with a son the same age, her instinct was to reach out to him. She touched his arm, and for a moment it felt solid and warm. She recalled thinking that the little boy could not possibly be a ghost because he was not cold, and from all that she had seen on television, ghosts were cold.

As she thought about this and watched the little boy, he unexpectedly jumped at her face, assuming a scary expression. Startled, but not really frightened, she covered her head for a moment, thinking the boy might be simply playing a game with her. When she peeked out from the covers, the boy was still there. Again she touched him, and again he quickly made a scary face. This time the guest carefully positioned the blanket in front of her face so she would not have to see the boy again and, after a few minutes, assumed he was gone. Then she felt movement on the blankets at the bottom of the bed. Spooked by what she had just experienced, she did not look to see what the movement was.

When she checked out of the hotel the next morning, the woman asked the desk clerk if anyone else had ever described anything like she had experienced the night before. She was not surprised to hear that others had seen the little boy, although the desk clerk told her that most of those sightings had occurred on the 12th floor.

Although they have a sense of humor, the Benson Hotel ghosts are friendly and helpful. Another guest, one with a disability, was having difficulty getting into bed one night when a porter appeared in front of her and gently assisted her into bed. When she turned to thank him for his kindness, however, he vanished before her eyes. No one has been able to describe well what the porter looks like, perhaps because he helps and vanishes so quickly, but he is known to assist guests in rooms when they need a helping hand.

The Lady in White is another helpful ghost. When she is not checking on guests, she wanders the floors and admires the decor.

The Lady in Blue is the ghost of a middle-aged woman who has been seen wearing a turquoise dress and bright red rings. She is a different form of apparition than the others, however, and people have reported seeing her only as a reflection in a lobby mirror looking back at them.

There have been other claims, not just of specific ghosts, but of voices, shadows, and even the sounds of ballroom music echoing through the halls in the middle of the night.

My stay on the seventh floor was not nearly as eventful as any of those. A paranormal researcher in the Benson Hotel is like a kid in a candy store, and we just can't wait for that moment when we get what we have waited for. Perhaps that was my problem. I wanted to see Simon Benson and his friends so badly that I may have inadvertently kept that from happening. I did, however, have the strong feeling of being watched on a few occasions and was awoken once by what I thought was the sound of something moving on the table. It was, quite possibly, a dream, but I would like to believe that it was one of the friendly residents of the hotel checking on me.

If you are looking for a beautiful and mysterious place to spend a night or two in the Portland area, I recommend the Benson Hotel, which has everything and more that you would expect from a fine luxury hotel. The rooms are not inexpensive, but they are not grossly overpriced either. Spend some time in the gym, enjoy dinner at the London Grill, and relax in your room with a few friendly ghosts. And say thank you to Simon Benson on your way out.

Cathedral Park

PORTLAND

TODAY, CATHEDRAL PARK in north Portland provides a breathtaking view of the towering St. Johns Bridge, nature, and the east shore of the Willamette River. Families often picnic there on sunny afternoons, the occasional wedding is held beneath the statuesque bridge, and the smell of trees and wildflowers add to the picture-perfect location. You could spend hours there, taking pictures and contemplating how little the scene has changed since the construction of the bridge in 1931. But times have changed, and most of the people who walked through Cathedral Park have faded into the past and are all but forgotten. All, perhaps, except for 15-year-old Thelma Taylor, who also thought the park was beautiful—until August 5, 1949, since which time the park has been haunted by stories of ghostly screams and shadowy figures.

Thelma was a sophomore at Roosevelt High School in Portland in the late 1940s. Thelma was not an unattractive girl but was teased in school for being skinny, among other things, and she did not have many friends. One can see Thelma sitting slightly away from the rest of her class at the end of the bottom row of her elementary school graduation picture, as if she did not belong with the rest of the children. That feeling of not quite fitting in followed Thelma throughout her short life, even as she grew into a beautiful young woman with dark hair and a brilliant, contagious smile.

Thelma was devoted to her family and did what she could to help them financially during the months away from school. In the summer of 1949, she took a job picking beans at a farm in nearby Hillsboro. She would rouse herself early in the morning and make her way to Cathedral Park, where a bus would stop to pick up those willing to spend the day working on the farm and then drop them back at the same spot late in the afternoon or early evening. But on August 5, Thelma never made it onto that bus.

There are many versions of what happened that morning, and it takes some time and research to separate truth from exaggeration. I have sifted through the myths and the ghost stories, and what follows is the truth as it appears in documents and legal records. But I must warn you that the facts are sometimes more frightening that the ghost stories. We can alter tales to fit our needs and situations, but the truth never changes.

Despite her best intentions, Thelma Taylor did not make it onto the bus that humid summer morning in 1949, and it departed without her because she was nowhere to be seen. She had been approached by a 22-year-old ex-convict named Morris Leland. To this day no one knows what Leland said or did to entice Thelma into following him away from the bus stop to the banks of the Willamette River beneath the St. Johns Bridge; it is one of the few questions that Morris Leland did not answer in the months and years to come. We know that Leland made sexual advances toward Thelma and that she vehemently refused them. And here is where the fine line between fact and fiction gets muddied. . . .

Thelma Taylor was not raped. Morris Leland's own words were, "I got scared because she was a good girl and would make trouble with the police." The rape scenario is what most people read about on ghost hunter websites, but the fact is that it simply did not happen. And it is important to me that we allow Thelma to maintain that small bit of her dignity.

Leland held Thelma near the riverbank throughout the night, well hidden in an area of thick underbrush. But when morning came and Thelma could hear the workers switching cars on a nearby railroad track, her first instinct was to scream for help. It was then, to avoid detection and certain arrest, that Leland struck Thelma in the head repeatedly with a steel bar. And then, to make sure she could not possibly scream for help again, he stabbed her, silencing her forever on that bank nearly eight blocks from Cathedral Park.

Leland threw the steel pipe and the knife into the river, hoping that the current would carry them far away, wiped his fingerprints from Thelma's lunch pail, gathered his cigarette butts, and buried Thelma in a shallow grave underneath a pile of driftwood on the riverbank.

Six days later, the Thursday, August 11, edition of the *Reading Eagle*, a Portland newspaper, reported that Morris Leland was arrested by Sergeant Vern Nicholson on suspicion of driving a stolen car and immediately blurted out a confession to the murder police did not even suspect at that time.

The police knew that Thelma Taylor, a 15-year-old farm worker, had been reported missing the previous Saturday by her parents when she did not return home. But there had been no evidence, no hint that she could have met with such a horrible demise.

"It is the most cold-blooded case I've ever had," said then-chief of detectives William Brown. His investigators reported that Leland confessed in detail that he had killed a young girl the previous Saturday. He then led police to the driftwood pile beneath St. Johns Bridge where he had hidden Thelma Taylor's body, and police found her there in the bobby socks, Levi's jeans, and plaid shirt that she had on when she left to catch the bus to Hillsboro. They also found her billfold, which contained her farm produce work cards and an invitation to Bible school. Thelma had been beaten about the head and stabbed twice.

"It's been on my mind ever since it happened," Leland said. He admitted to picking Thelma up early on Friday morning as she waited for the bus and to holding her all night and day in the thicket on the bank of the river. He was no stranger to the system, having already served two penitentiary terms for conspiracy to commit a felony and for obtaining money under false pretenses in his scant 22 years, and he also had an extensive juvenile record. Now he was indicted for first-degree murder.

Morris Leland's trial began on October 4, 1950, and he entered a plea of not guilty by reason of insanity. But after a four-month trial, Leland was found guilty of the murder of Thelma Taylor and, on February 7, 1951, was sentenced to death. Morris Leland was led to the gas chamber, and his sentence was carried out in January 1953.

To those who know the story of Thelma Taylor, the Cathedral Park area is a place where innocence lived and died, where an evil man claimed an innocent life and spent his last days of freedom.

I have visited Cathedral Park on many occasions. During the day it is a beautiful area, surrounded by trees, the sound of the Willamette River, children laughing, and couples walking their dogs. If you stop to ask people if they know of Thelma Taylor, most locals tell you yes, and even many visitors know her story. And it is easy to talk about during the daytime. But when darkness falls, the feeling in the park changes. Perhaps this is because I know about Thelma. Or, perhaps, the stories of spectral screams and ghostly shadows hold some truth to them.

Over the decades, many people have reported hearing a young girl's voice calling, "Help! Somebody help me, please!" Cathedral Park is a hangout after dark for the younger generation who want to party, have a few beers, and the like, so many of those stories must be questioned, if only because alcohol is involved. But it is not only inebriated young people who have reported the ghostly voices and apparitions that they say dart quickly around the place.

Many paranormal researchers say that the area surrounding Cathedral Park has been primed for a haunting, and the flowing water of the river and the limestone blocks used to build St. Johns Bridge all are associated with a "residual haunting." Residual haunting is a new term made popular by paranormal television for an old parapsychological theory proposed in the 1970s called the Stone Tape theory. This theory speculates that inanimate materials, such as stone, can absorb energy from the living, much as a tape recorder absorbs the voice of the living, especially during episodes of high tension, anxiety, and fear. Once this energy is stored, it can also be released, resulting in the display, or replay, of the recorded events.

"We have to postulate that some very emotional scene has somehow become registered on the environment, almost like a sort of psychic video has been created," late Scottish paranormal researcher Archie Roy was quoted as saying about Stone Tape theory in the 2011 book *Ghosts* by Malcolm Day. "Someone who comes along who is sensitive enough acts as a sort of psychic video player and will actually play that 'tape' and see the figures or perhaps even hear the voices."

One has to wonder if this is what has been happening for nearly seven decades in Cathedral Park, especially when hundreds of visitors all claim to see and hear the same thing.

Remaining in Cathedral Park after dark did not frighten me as much as it saddened me. Even as my digital voice recorder ran, and the flash of my camera shed some light on the scenery, I thought about Thelma. At one point I did hear a young woman's voice whisper two words near me. I could not make them out, nor did they appear on my voice recorder; the wind and rain made practically all of my audio recordings and still photography from that visit useless. But I did not feel alone while I was there, and I did not feel threatened. I have been asked if I thought the voice I heard was Thelma's, and I do—not because I know what Thelma sounded like, not because I heard any specific words, but because my instincts tell me it was. And as any true paranormal researcher will tell you, your instinct is one of your best tools.

To this day, the Portland Police Department receives random phone calls reporting a woman screaming for help in Cathedral Park, but each time police arrive to neither see nor hear anything.

Thelma's family held no grudges toward her murderer, and my instinct tells me that neither does she. Coming from such a loving family could only have produced a loving, beautiful young woman.

I suggest a visit to this historic area to anyone visiting the Portland area, especially if you seek to delve a bit into paranormal reports and activity. Enjoy the park and the Gothic-style St. Johns Bridge during the day. And be sure to say hello to Thelma after the sun goes down.

CHAPTER 4

ComedySportz
PORTLAND

WHEN MOST PEOPLE THINK of a comedy club, they do not necessarily liken it to a boxing match or mixed martial arts bout. But ComedySportz in Portland has quite a bit in common with both.

A boxing or MMA match has two competitors, a referee, and a panel of judges. The competitors battle it out to be the best and hopefully win, the referee is on hand to call out fouls or illegal actions, and the panel of judges ultimately decides the winner. ComedySportz has two competitors (two comedy teams), a referee, and a panel of judges. Each team battles it out with hilarious jokes, skits, and songs. The referee is on hand to call foul, to relay suggestions from the audience, and to keep things moving right along. The panel of judges—which, in this case, is the audience—decides the winner of the bout via applause. It is a high-energy, fast-paced show that leaves spectators rolling in the aisles.

Another thing people do not necessarily associate with a comedy show is ghosts, but ComedySportz entertains in more than one way. It provides laughs, good company, and a family-friendly environment, and it also includes a paranormal element with its resident ghost—a spirit that apparently enjoys the shows as well!

The history of ComedySportz goes back 30 years to Milwaukee, Wisconsin, and a gentleman named Dick Chudnow. With a different structure than most comedy clubs, ComedySportz took off almost immediately, and another venue opened a year later in Madison, Wisconsin. Three years later, the first Comedy League of America National Tournament was held in Madison, with 10 teams participating. The World Comedy League now has more than 20 teams from as far away as the United Kingdom and Germany, proving hands down that laughter is a universal language.

ComedySportz came to Portland in 1993 with Ruth Jenkins and Patrick Short, who are not only performers but are also the club president and general manager, respectively. Their run in Portland has been impressive, with more than 3,000 shows in 18 seasons and never missing a weekend. Unlike most comedy clubs, ComedySportz is family friendly, with children of all ages welcome at the shows. It is not out of the ordinary to see 4-year-old children sitting next to 40-year-old adults, enjoying the laughs, smiles, and ongoing entertainment.

One has to wonder why more ghosts do not haunt comedy clubs. . . . What better place to spend eternity? Instead of hanging out in dark, dingy rooms or deserted hospitals, wouldn't life after death be more fun with unlimited laughter and happy people? If I have a choice after I die, you will find my ghost at ComedySportz.

It seems that one woman did decide to remain at Comedy-Sportz, and over the years a number of people have seen the specter of a middle-aged woman with red hair and a contagious laugh. The ComedySportz ghost seems to especially enjoy spending time in the costume closet and with movie outfits. Objects often get moved from one place to another, and a quiet voice has been heard both throughout the building and in the costume closet in particular. If she is attempting to attract someone's attention, she will knock on doors or walls or other solid objects to indicate she is there. She has also been known to flip on and off the lights and laugh hysterically.

No area of ComedySportz is off-limits for its mischievous ghost, including the bathroom. There are dozens of reports of toilets flushing on their own, either while the bathroom is unoccupied or while customers are in the privacy of a stall. Hearing a toilet flush on its own can be a bit unnerving to most people, but it has become part of the ghost's charm and practical-joking sense of humor. Those who have experienced this particular form of paranormal activity warn that it is best to finish what they went into the bathroom for before running to an awaiting public.

I didn't experience any of this while I was there and was honestly too busy laughing and pounding on my table. Most of the people I spoke with after the show were much like me in that they were laughing too hard to take notice of much else. But there are some who visit ComedySportz on a regular basis who have heard the ghostly woman's laughter and her knocks for attention, and a few who have experienced her bathroom pranks.

"I come in sometimes for the workshops or other things they have going on here," said one young woman. "It's much quieter during the day when there are no shows going on. I have heard her laughing and knocking on things. It's not scary or anything. It's neat that someone would want to hang out here after they died. I bet she was an awesome, funny person when she was alive!"

I also spoke with a young man who volunteers at Comedy-Sportz who has not only heard the laughter but seen lights go on and off for no apparent reason.

"I was by myself in a room the first time it happened, and it creeped me out," he told me. "I was talking to myself, trying to calm down. Then I thought, 'This is stupid, it's just a light. It's not like Freddy Krueger or anything!' It's happened a few times. There aren't electrical problems at all. Just off and on. I think the ghost likes it here and likes to joke around. It's not like ghosts you see in the movies or anything. It's just interesting and fun after you get used to it."

Not one person I spoke with felt any fear of the happy ghost that resides at ComedySportz. Most seem to know about her and simply consider her to be part of the audience and the Comedy-Sportz family. And judging from the many reports of her hysterical laughter, she obviously appreciates the comedic talent that abounds at the club.

ComedySportz is proof that haunted locations do not have to be dark and frightening, spine tingling, or traumatizing, and I highly recommend catching a show while you are in Portland. I have always believed that we are in death what we were in life, that we carry our personalities with us, and if this is true, then this particular ghost is happy and content where she is.

ComedySportz offers much more than comedy shows each week, including a number of workshops and classes. One of the top eight comedy schools in the nation, ComedySportz holds improv classes for both adults and youth, stand-up comedy classes, team building and applied improvisation for businesses, and a number of other ways to learn how to keep oneself and others laughing and entertained.

ComedySportz is also community oriented and gives back in many ways. It sets aside 15% of its pretax profits each year and chooses a charity to donate it to; some of the charities it has helped include the American Red Cross, Oregon Humane Society, Oregon Special Olympics, Oregon Food Bank, and Camp

Ukandu. ComedySportz makes people all over Oregon and across the country smile in many different ways.

ComedySportz provides a good example of ghosts not being the spooky, frightening entities we are used to seeing on paranormal reality television. In fact, in my experience, the spooky, frightening ghosts are the exception. What we often forget is that any ghost was once as alive as you and I and had families, friends, emotions, and unique personalities. I believe that these traits are carried over when we pass; the energy that we carry as we live only changes forms when we die. I often recall the quote from Patrick Swayze's character Sam Wheat in the movie *Ghost*: "It's amazing, Molly. The love inside . . . we take it with us. . . ." That's the truest reference to life after death I have heard.

And in the case of the ghost at ComedySportz, she took to the other side her love for laughter and passion for practical jokes.

CHAPTER 5

Heathman Hotel
PORTLAND

BUILT IN 1927, the Heathman Hotel was designed specifically to provide a grand lodging environment to lumber magnates, railroad tycoons, and the excessively wealthy. Those that held this privileged status came to expect accommodations and services that were on a higher level than those available to the ordinary working man, and the Heathman obliged. Today it is yet another downtown Portland landmark hotel that boasts numerous ghosts and hauntings.

The hotel's grand opening after seven months of construction received public laurels and acclaim and was quite the elaborate celebration. Oregon governor I. L. Patterson and mayor of
Portland George Luis Baker attended and made jubilant dedica-
tion speeches. Local radio station KOIN pitched in with a live
band and a grand orchestra section. City commissioners, businessmen, and residents alike joined the festivities, paying tribute to Portland's newest, and some say finest, hotel.

The *Oregon Journal* continued the ovation by devoting several stories and columns to "Oregon's newest and most modern
hotel." Its coverage of the Heathman included statements such
as "planning, construction, and general appointments are as
modern as human ingenuity and talent could possibly make it"
and "located on Broadway . . . ablaze with theatre marquees, restaurants, and shops." And, indeed, the Heathman was a sight to
behold, with huge, bold marquee lights surrounding the 10-story
building, and it was destined to become the main attraction of
downtown Portland's entertainment epicenter.

In the 1950s, the Broadway District suffered when many
businesses and entertainment venues left for the newly booming suburbs, and by the mid-1960s, the glory that had been
reserved for the Heathman and its neighboring establishments
had faded, losing their appeal to newcomers to the area. By the
1970s, newly elected city leaders saw what the downtown area
of Portland had once been and felt it was a worthy project to
attempt to bring back the enchantment of the area by enticing
retail stores and other businesses to either keep their existing
locations downtown or build new establishments. The Seattle
group Paramount Northwest took the first steps to rebuild and
reintroduce the district with the old Paramount Theater next
door to the Heathman in 1972, and the Portland City Council
voted to give the neglected theater landmark status. By 1976,
West Coast Theaters purchased the Paramount, and today a

performing arts center known as the Arlene Schnitzer Concert Hall is still a popular entertainment venue.

With the 1980s came a cultural renaissance that breathed life back into the downtown Portland area and the Heathman Hotel. Once again, the hotel became an important part of Broadway, along with the theater and culture districts, and it came to life again, from the inside out.

Andrew Delfina, an acclaimed interior designer, worked with granite, marble, and teak to bring back the interior splendor of the Heathman. The restoration of the hotel's exterior and its eucalyptus-paneled Tea Court brought it to the attention of many, and soon after the Heathman was recognized as a National Historic Landmark. A few more years and $16 million dollars later, the restoration was complete, and the Heathman Hotel reopened in 1984 in its entire original splendor.

But there was still room for improvement, and in 2002, more renovations were underway at the Heathman. At the finish of this phase, the lobby displayed jaw-dropping Art Deco designs of the 1920s combined with Japanese decorative elements. Today the hotel boasts a remarkable art collection, with works from the 18th century to Andy Warhol.

Another amenity that the Heathman offers that very few hotels do is a library, and it is one of the most extensive guest libraries in the country and includes more than 2,000 volumes, most signed by the authors and displayed beautifully in custom cases on the mezzanine. The lavish collection even includes rare, signed editions from Pulitzer Prize winners, US poet laureates, and two US presidents. Many notable writers have visited and stayed at the Heathman over the decades— Stephen King, John Updike, Jimmy Carter, Bill Clinton, and James Patterson, to name just a few—and they have left behind autographed works to share with other guests in the ever-growing library.

Rooms at the Heathman rage from 260 square feet to 600 square feet and are designed for visual pleasure as well as comfort. Many boast in-room fireplaces, choice of mattresses from the hotel's "art of sleep" menu, and unique decor from local artists. It truly is an experience that visitors do not soon forget.

But there is a more supernatural side to the Heathman that centers on the multifloor column of rooms that end in the number 3, and all of those rooms have been the subject of reports of unexplained activity.

If you ask old-timers about ghosts at the Heathman, you will most likely hear stories of rooms 703, 803, and 1003 which are said to be the "column rooms" that were quickly passed as a distraught former guests fell or jumped to their deaths. Celebrity psychic Sylvia Browne reportedly visited the Heathman in 1999, staying in one of the column rooms, room 803, and upon her arrival immediately saw a ghost at the end of her bed. Her feeling during the communication with this spirit was that someone over the years had jumped to his death from the top of the Heathman and continues to haunt the rooms he passed on his way down.

When the Heathman Hotel was being built it was the largest construction project of its time in Portland.

Others claim to see the apparition of George Heathman Jr., who was responsible for the construction and operation of both the Heathman Hotel and the Roosevelt Hotel, located two blocks away. He passed away less than three years after the completion of the Heathman at the age of just 49, and many feel that he has remained behind because he was not finished with his business.

One employee says he has seen Mr. Heathman on numerous occasions near the front desk and in the library. While he is generally not afraid of the apparition, he said, it is unnerving when he witnesses it alone.

"Most of the time there are a few of us and we all see it," he told me. "It's not really like seeing a ghost. He is very solid, very real, until he just vanishes in front of our eyes. That feeling . . . it's kind of uneasy. I have read up on things like residual hauntings [and] this isn't just the remnant of George. He actually will turn and look us right in the eyes. Sometimes he is with a younger guy that we think is his son. Sometimes he will smile a little. I take that to mean we are doing a good job. At least I hope that is what he means by it!"

Many have also seen a female spirit, as well as another male spirit that does not look like George Heathman. The female is well dressed in the style of the 1950s, and the other, the employees say, is "more hip, like the '60s."

The female is often seen in many of the same areas where guests and employees have reported seeing George Heathman.

"Just hanging out. Very pleasant looking and sweet looking," an employee told me. "I hear stories all the time, and there have been a few times people have just left during the night or first thing in the morning. Usually they have stayed in the column. The ghost in the column scares people. George doesn't, but the ghost in the column has a totally different feel."

Research turns up no documented cases of suicide by jumping at the Heathman, but that is not unusual. Many times, especially in high-end hotels, these things just did not occur—even if they did. But the female ghost and the other male ghost may well be George Heathman Jr.'s wife, Katherine, and son Harry. Both were invested financially and emotionally in the hotel, and Harry managed the establishment until shortly before his death in 1962. The Heathman Hotel, by all accounts, was their pride and joy, and they devoted their lives to keeping it true to George's dream.

Guests have reported seeing Katherine in their rooms as they got into bed, as though she is ensuring their comfort, and often in the library with George. They report a woman with a pleasant smile and never for a moment feel threatened or overly frightened.

"I was startled but not scared when I saw her in my room," one guest told me during my visit. "It seemed like we looked at each other for a long time, but it was actually probably just a matter of 30 or 40 seconds before she just floated away. She didn't walk, she floated. I am hoping I get to see her again! It was easily the best part of this vacation."

I was interested in hearing about the ghosts of the Heathman family, but I must admit I really wanted to know more about the ghost in the column. While it is worth every penny, the Heathman was a bit out of my budget for a room, but I did take a brief tour of the column rooms. And while I cannot say that I saw anything I would deem paranormal, I did get an overwhelming feeling in 703 that I was being watched closely. The hair on the back of my neck actually stood on end. Another indication to me that something was slightly out of the ordinary was the pockets of cold air where there was no source for them. It was there, then it was gone, only to have moved a few feet in either direction.

I am by no means a psychic or a medium, but I sometimes am able to get brief flashes, like a Polaroid snapshot; this is rare for me, but it does happen occasionally. I never heard a name, but I saw two brief flashes of a signature of a first name, Robert. With

30 years in the paranormal research field, I am the first to tell you that this is not evidence. Personal experiences are just that: personal. But they are something to build on for future research.

Based on what people told me and on my own experiences, I believe the Heathman family remains at the hotel that gave them such joy in life. It is not uncommon for those who have passed to remain at a location that was near and dear to their hearts, or to at least pay the occasional visit. By all accounts the ghosts of George and Katherine seem pleased with what they see and those they choose to appear to. To me, the word *haunting*, while accurate, does not fit this particular location; it is more of a case of the owner-builder-manager checking in to oversee the hotel he watched grow from the foundation up. And his reported smile would seem to indicate his pride.

The column ghost is quite another story. It is entirely possible that someone jumped from the higher floors of the Heathman. Many wealthy men lost their life savings during the Great Depression, and suicides were commonplace during that time. And it is not unusual for a suicide not to have been reported as such, perhaps in an attempt to allow the deceased to go without disgrace. But my feeling is that the man in 703 is not happy in death and may be trapped and seeking a way out. We will likely never know. We know only that hundreds of people who have stayed at the Heathman have encountered this man and have used such words to describe him as *brooding, sad, lonely,* and *desperate*. Maybe someone reading this right now will be the next person he reaches out to.

So be sure to visit the Heathman Hotel while you are in Portland if you can. Whatever your desire, rest assured that the Heathman will try to accommodate it. And they will even provide the ghosts free of charge!

CHAPTER 6

Hollywood Theatre
PORTLAND

THE 1920S WERE AN INNOVATIVE TIME for the movie industry with the transition from silent films to talkies. Theaters became more than just dark rooms with chairs and screens on the walls; they evolved into elaborate palaces that allowed the moviegoer a temporary escape from everyday life.

They were luxurious, decorative, often everything that working class families could not experience in their own homes, and for an hour or two, those people became movie stars and part of the story. The Hollywood Theatre was a big part of that era in Portland.

At 2 p.m. on Saturday, July 17, 1926, with a line of waiting patrons wrapping around the block, the Hollywood Theatre publicly opened the doors to its 1,500 seats for the first time with the showing of *More Pay—Less Work*.

A local advertisement for the theater called it a "palace of luxury, comfort and entertainment unsurpassed by any theatre on the Coast." Constructed during the silent film era, the Hollywood was not without sounds of drama, comedy, and laughter, and was the last theater built to provide a stage to both vaudeville acts and films, with accompaniment by an eight-piece orchestra and an organist.

The majestic appearance of the Hollywood was the product of a Portland design firm called Bennes & Herzog, and their artistic liberties are a sight to behold to this day. Some have described the look of the Hollywood as Byzantine, but it is, more accurately, a Spanish Colonial Revival design. Spanish Colonial Revival architecture began in the early 20th century, inspired by the architecture brought to the Americas from Spain. Buildings constructed in this style often boast tile roofs, rustic wood beams, arches, tile work, white stucco, and ornate detailing on the doors. The Hollywood's intricate details still shine brightly through its century-old outer walls, and were it not for the theater marquee, you might think for a moment that you were standing before an ornate church.

Outwardly the Hollywood has not changed much since 1926, but its heart has continued to advance with the times and, as the film industry changed, so did the technical capabilities of the theater. Cinerama was introduced to the public in the late 1950s, and it was only a few years before the Hollywood adapted to the new way of projecting films and became the first Cinerama theater in the Northwest. Cinerama required three separate projectors and a larger wraparound screen to achieve its full effect. People entering the Hollywood to see a movie may notice two small, closetlike rooms on either side of the theater, which were used to project films in Cinerama.

More changes came in the 1970s when the theater was divided into three separate auditoriums, a main one with 394 seats, a second with 114, and a third with 111, allowing the Hollywood to show three different films simultaneously. This was also groundbreaking, as it predated cinema multiplexes.

Despite the attention the theater received when it was listed in the National Register of Historic Places in 1983, the Hollywood became a victim to the newer and more modern theaters in Portland, and its business all but disappeared. Few people wanted to see new action or science fiction films with state-of-the-art special effects in an old theater that was once the home to vaudeville acts and silent movies. Once a literal entertainment palace, the Hollywood was reduced to showing second-run discount movies. A Portland legend appeared to have come to a sad end.

But in the 21st century, the Hollywood came back to life. It now not only shows movies but also focuses on independent and local filmmakers and educational programs. No one can accuse the Hollywood of not being able to adjust with the times, and because of that, its legacy lives on. And so do the ghosts that reside there.

To anyone visiting the Hollywood Theatre for the first time, it can feel a bit surreal. Perhaps this is because of its location, which is not the bustling part of Portland that it once was, and while one can almost feel the historic energy from the theater, everything around it seems strangely subdued. The Hollywood

Burger Bar is just down the block, and an Irish gift shop, a liquor and discount cigarette store, and a check-cashing establishment are nearby. The businesses themselves seem quiet as well, but maybe it is just that everything pales in comparison to the Hollywood.

Walking into the theater for the first time was an almost dreamlike experience for me. I am fascinated by history and architecture, so I found the best of both worlds in the lobby of the Hollywood. While parts of the theater have been updated with modern amenities, I could still envision vaudeville acts and silent movies and Model T Fords parked outside. I recall beginning almost every sentence directed to my companions with "Can you almost see it?" or "Can you imagine?" The history was alive.

The ghosts of the Hollywood have never been given obligatory names or identified as other than male and female, but the reports of their existence are many. Past theater managers recall seeing a well-dressed, middle-aged man floating or hovering in the upstairs lobby. Some people have reported seeing a young, blonde female in high heels in the upstairs theater. She has also been seen nervously pacing the halls while smoking a cigarette. The sightings are brief but detailed, and each witness recalls a similar experience. People also report a feeling of uneasiness on the stairs leading to the upper theaters. A male ghost enjoys tapping people on the shoulder or back and whispering unintelligible words into their ears. Yet another ghost, a female, has been seen sitting quietly in the back row of the theater.

One might well wonder if these are the ghosts of vaudevillian performers who were not quite ready to move aside for the magic of motion pictures. Many who have encountered the ghost that lingers on the stairs, tapping and whispering, feel he was a vaudeville performer. While many are startled by a physical touch, most feel that it is done in jest. In all of the accounts that have been relayed to me, no one has felt threatened or fearful.

"If I could have seen him, I would have poked him back!" one older gentleman told me with a laugh.

A woman I spoke with after my visit who claimed to be a medium said that the nervously pacing female ghost waits eternally for her husband to pick her up from work, not knowing he had been killed in an automobile accident on the way to meet her. I do not have an opinion either way on mediums or psychics, and this explanation certainly seems plausible when I consider the reports and the repetitive actions of this particular ghost, but we will never know if this is indeed true.

There does not seem to be any rhyme or reason to the floating man or the woman seen in the back rows. Perhaps they simply enjoyed their time at the Hollywood and thought it would be a nice place to retire after they expired. But turning from a conversation there, I caught a glimpse of a misty, transparent figure that passed before me and dissolved into the wall. It was not as detailed as many other reports, but I do not doubt what I saw with my own eyes. I replay it over and over in my mind in an attempt to come up with a rational, natural explanation, but am left without one.

As the sun began to set, the mood of the theater seemed to change, and at one point I was actually eager to leave. Two people in my party heard a voice whisper "Hey, you!" and felt unexplained cold spots that had not been there before. It seemed as though when the darkness set in, people we were not able to see were arriving to watch their favorite movies. And perhaps that was the case, nothing more and nothing less.

As we pulled away from the Hollywood Theatre, the thought that kept repeating itself in my mind was that history never dies. The past is alive. The present is merely lived.

Lone Fir Pioneer Cemetery
PORTLAND

LONE FIR PIONEER CEMETERY sits between Stark Street to the north and Morrison Street to the south. It is the oldest cemetery in the Portland area and the largest one managed by regional government. It covers more than 30 acres and is home to more than 25,000 gravesites, and as a result of negligent maintenance and record keeping over the years, those buried within 10,000 of them are unknown. Oftentimes no one documented the paupers when they were interred.

If there was ever a cemetery that was ripe for hauntings, it would be Lone Fir. Unmarked graves of insane asylum patients, a notorious murderess, graves lost in the shuffle of combining other cemeteries with Lone Fir, and possibly even graves that have not yet been discovered.

The first official burial at Lone Fir was in 1846, when Emmon Stephens was buried on a plot of land that once belonged to his neighbor, a gentleman by the name of Seldon Murray. A decade later, Murray sold Stephens's gravesite and the adjacent 10 acres to Colburn Barrell with the stipulation that his friend's grave be tended to. Barrell agreed and kept his word. Not long after this transfer of property, the cemetery was born.

Barrell owned a steamboat on the Willamette River called the *Gazelle*. In 1856 the *Gazelle* exploded near Oregon City and killed Barrell's business partner, Crawford Dobbins, as well as a passenger. The 10 acres that were purchased from Seldon Murray would now be known as Mount Crawford Cemetery, after Barrell's deceased business partner, who was interred there along with the passenger.

By 1866, Barrell added 20 acres to the cemetery and sold burial plots for $10 each. Later that same year, Barrell realized that the upkeep of a cemetery was more work than he could

"He endured the adventures of the plains and mountains and here," reads the gravestone of Asa Lovejoy at Lone Fir Pioneer Cemetery.

handle, and he offered to sell Mount Crawford to the city of Port-land, which quickly declined. So Barrell sold the cemetery to a group of private investors for a tidy sum of money instead. Those investors immediately renamed the cemetery Lone Fir in honor of the single, lone fir tree that stood at the location.

But the investors had no practical idea of how to maintain a cemetery. Lone Fir fell into a sad state of disrepair. By the late 1920s, the gravesites, thousands of them unknown, were hidden beneath prickly mounds of blackberry vines and other invasive species. A few stone markers were still there, but the majority of the wooden markers had succumbed to rot or one of the many fires that swept through the area.

In 1928, Multnomah County took over control and mainte-nance of Lone Fir and, in 1947, paved over a large part of the cemetery and built an office on the site. Sadly, the portion paved over was the burial site for many Chinese immigrants; these remains were removed the following year and are said to have been sent back to China. In 2004 more graves were discovered beneath the office site. It was not until 2007 that the office build-ing was removed and more Chinese immigrant remains were found. That same year Lone Fir was added to the National Reg-ister of Historic Places.

Today the cemetery is in the capable and caring hands of Friends of Lone Fir Cemetery, which has brought new interest and vitality to it and removed the stigma often associated with such places. This organization has made Lone Fir a fun learn-ing experience for visitors of all ages and offers tours, concerts to raise funds for headstones that have been vandalized, plays, scavenger hunts, and even Scrabble tournaments. It also runs a family-friendly Halloween event called Graveyard Goodies that it describes as a "trick-or-treating party featuring some of Lone Fir Cemetery's most prominent ghosts." The ghosts are actors, and visitors of all ages converse with the prominent residents, doctors, and laborers whose names have been lost or were never known. There is no need to go door-to-door for candy because the "ghosts" hand it out—and they even give autographs.

Anyone who knows a bit about the city's sordid history will surely recognize a name or two at the cemetery—and even if they do not, chances are they will want to research a few after visiting Lone Fir. People from every walk of life—the famous, the insane, the freed slaves, the leaders in science—can be found at Lone Fir.

A white obelisk honors Dr. James C. Hawthorne, who was in charge of an insane asylum in the 1800s. Dr. Hawthorne genuinely cared for his patients, even when their families had long forgotten about them. Many times a family would not bother to claim the bodies of the deceased, so Dr. Hawthorne buried more than 130 of his patients at Lone Fir at his own expense. It is not known exactly where the former patients are buried, but it is speculated that they were interred in what is called Block 14 in the southwest corner of the cemetery. Block 14 is also the site of unmarked graves of numerous Chinese railroad workers.

Another notable resident of Lone Fir is Charity Lamb, who murdered her husband in 1854. Nathaniel Lamb sat at the dinner table as he usually did, entertaining his children with animated stories, when Charity quietly stepped up behind him and brought an ax down against the back of his head. Twice. Even more amazing is that Nathaniel lived for two weeks before he gave up the ghost and succumbed to the ax wounds. Charity Lamb was the first woman to be convicted of murder in the Oregon Territory. She did not receive the death penalty but was instead sentenced to a lifetime of hard labor at the Oregon State Penitentiary in 1854. A decade later, she was transferred to Dr. Hawthorne's insane asylum, where she died in 1879. And so she ended up near Dr. Hawthorne in life and in death.

Not much is known about Michael Mitchell, a dancer in Portland and who froze to death on the steps of his boardinghouse.

Some say he was intoxicated and not allowed inside while under the influence. But what a shock it must have been for other boarders to emerge from the house the next morning to find him frozen and stiff on the front stoop!

Not long ago, a gentleman and his friend decided to check out Lone Fir after dark. Walking along the roadside, the pair explored the cemetery, looking at names on the headstones, when one man looked up and saw a figure standing about 50 yards away from them. He called out to the figure but received no response. His first thought was that someone had seen them and was trying to frighten them. So they walked toward the figure, playing along with the spooky prank.

As they approached, the figure seemed to jerk its head upward to the sky, just staring, and they realized that they might not be dealing with a joke after all. The figure was obscured by the trees, but as they cautiously moved closer, they could make out the face of an elderly man with a long beard, wearing a white shirt and black pants. They shouted hello, and in response, the man violently jerked his head toward them, opened his mouth, and screamed. The men say the figure's eyes were blank as it continued to stare at them before letting go with another loud scream. After seeing the man's weird eyes and hearing the second scream, the two of them left the cemetery in a hurry and have never been back.

No one else I spoke with reported anything nearly so frightening, and most described seeing misty figures walking across the cemetery during the daytime as well as after dark. Visitors repeatedly see a younger woman in a red dress who seems to be happily strolling through the grounds, oblivious to anyone around her.

My visit to Lone Fir was during the daytime and, due to rain, not as long as I would have liked. Unfortunately, I did not spot the woman in the red dress or the zombie-like specter that the men saw. Occasionally I felt as though I was being watched, but not to the point that it caused me any concern or fear. After all, I was a guest in the home of those who are buried there, and I expected to be watched.

Lone Fir Pioneer Cemetery is beautiful, even in the rain. The stately obelisks and headstones with photographs are almost breathtaking. You can feel a connection with some who are interred there because many headstones contain more information than any I have ever seen.

One in particular that I was fascinated with was the headstone for James B. and Elizabeth Stephens, who were early pioneers in the area. James B. Stephens's father was Emmon Stephens, the first man buried on the property.

Theirs is not your normal headstone. The images of Mr. and Mrs. Stephens are carved into the headstone in a realistic style. On the back of the marker is a stone that, to me, was touching.

"Here we lie by consent after 57 years, two months, two days sojourning on earth awaiting nature's immutable laws to return us to the elements of which we were formed," the inscription reads.

You can't pass up the Soldier's Monument, which memorializes the Indian Wars, Mexican-American War, American Civil War, and Spanish-American War. It was constructed in 1903 with $3,500 in community donations and is a beautiful, stately memorial that stands strong and proud to this day.

When people ask me if Lone Fir Pioneer Cemetery is haunted, I have to answer, "How could it not be?" With its tragedies and thousands of forgotten graves, lost ghosts likely wander the cemetery. And whether visitors want to participate in an event or hope to catch a glimpse of a ghost, they will leave with a new knowledge of the people who were essential in making Portland the city it is today, so it is definitely worth a trip. When you find yourself in Portland, you can stop by and judge for yourself.

CHAPTER 8

Oaks Park

PORTLAND

AMERICA'S OLDEST CONTINUALLY OPERATING
amusement park is in Portland, yet even those who have lived in
the area are sometimes unaware of its existence.

Oaks Amusement Park opened on May 30, 1905, just two
days before the famous Lewis and Clark Exposition, and was
immediately dubbed the Coney Island of the Northwest. Thousands of tourists from around the United States and the world
flocked to Portland's first and only World's Fair to be a part of the
city's celebration. Executives at the Portland Railway, Light, and
Power Company, which owned the property on which Oaks Park
was built and the trolley lines leading out to it, were keeping
their fingers crossed that overflow from the exposition would

send tourists in their direction, and it did. People left the fair, headed straight for Oaks Park, and were fascinated by the new-fangled carnival rides there. They bought tickets and lined up yards deep for the giant Ferris wheel, the twists and turns of the roller coaster, and the gentle serenity of the carousel. Most of the new contraptions would soon become mainstays in amusement parks around the world, but for the time being, people were see-ing them for the first time and taking full advantage of their newness and excitement.

They were also making Oaks Park's first few days extremely profitable ones. The venture remained profitable for years, despite admission being a mere dime and trolley rides just a nickel. The Oaks Amusement Park was on the map.

Portland Railway, Light, and Power Company's goal was to increase the number of people who rode the streetcars from Portland to up-and-coming towns like Gresham, Estacada, and Oregon City, and it accomplished this early on. But one man, theater and museum owner John Cordray, wanted something more for Oaks Park. With high hopes he leased the park from the power company when laws were enacted to prevent utility companies from owning amusement parks, and he set to work on accomplishing his dream. For the next 16 years he monopo-lized the amusement and entertainment revenues in Portland.

Cordray brought so much more than carnival rides to the Oaks. There was the bathhouse for swimming, a beautifully composed picnic area, concerts and theater productions, chorus girls, and spirits and libations. But the most jaw-dropping and thrilling ride was Chute the Chutes, a two-story waterslide that was the first of its kind. And for more mature visitors, there was the Mystic River, a floating tunnel of love where gentlemen suit-ors could attempt a quick kiss from the objects of their affections. He even set aside days to bring in children who were housed in charitable institutions so that they, too, might enjoy the splendor that the Oaks had to offer, and they left with their baskets and bags filled with sandwiches, candy, and treats.

Then, in 1908, alcohol was banned at the Oaks. Many say the decision to do away with alcohol was not Cordray's preference but was insisted upon after a fatal accident. In the summer of that year, an intoxicated 23-year-old named David Smith tried to jump aboard the streetcar, lost his grip, and fell to the tracks, where his head was crushed by the trolley wheels, killing him instantly.

But this tragedy was a temporary setback for the Oaks, and it was soon forgotten amid the laughter and smiles. Before long the park was once again booming with activity and profit.

In 1925, John Cordray passed away unexpectedly. After an appropriate length of time for mourning, his widow sold the Oaks to Edward Bollinger and his son, Robert. The Bollingers were just as enthusiastic about the park as Cordray had been, and some say even more dedicated. Their creative marketing abilities and masterful expertise when it came to upgrading the park's attractions earned the Oaks the title of the longest continually running amusement park in America.

The Bollingers added even more thrilling rides to the park— the Giant Whirl, Dodgem Cars, the Laughing Gallery, Mystic Maze, and the popular Figure Eight roller coaster.

Competition to the Oaks came in 1928 with the opening of Jantzen Beach Amusement Company in North Portland. But the Oaks persevered over the decades that followed, and the new park was razed and replaced by a shopping mall in the 1970s. The Oaks survived natural disasters and tragedies and never stopped building new attractions and arcade games.

More than 100 years of history lives on at the Oaks Amusement Park, although as a result of the Willamette River flooding in 1913, 1948, and 1996 the only original buildings still intact are the dance hall and the skating rink.

Robert Bollinger continued to successfully operate the Oaks after his father's death, and in 1985 he created a nonprofit organization to oversee the duties, operations, and funding of the park, ensuring its perpetual success. Today the Oaks Amusement Park is a physical manifestation of the Bollingers' dream, and fun is still had by all.

One might not expect a happy place like the Oaks to be haunted, but history itself is a ghost, and so there might not be a better place for spirits to reside.

The last time I visited the Oaks I spoke with an old-timer who was employed by the park during the 1950s and 1960s. He relayed not only the tragic story of David Smith but also that of a young girl, probably about 9 years old, who was visiting the park for the first time and was very excited. She ran ahead of her parents after arriving and tripped, hitting her head and dying instantly without ever experiencing the park. My source teared up a bit as he recalled this story, and I had no reason to doubt his honesty and accuracy. It would explain the many visitors who, especially after dark, see a young, sad-looking girl in period clothing from the 1920s or 1930s standing quietly in the picnic area or near the carousel, there one moment and gone the next. The accounts that I heard all had one detail in common, and that was that she had a big white bow in her hair. And on quiet evenings in the park, or after closing, many have reported hearing the sobs of a young girl or quiet footsteps following them, and perhaps this is the spirit of the child who never quite made it into the park.

Others have reported seeing a young man, quite possibly the ghost of David Smith, wandering the grounds as if he were lost. Most reports say he never appears fully solid, but rather transparent and in shades of gray. He, too, has a tendency to follow people around the park, guests and employees alike. Sometimes they only hear heavy footsteps, and other times they are accompanied by whispers or flashes of light.

Many guests have also reported seeing floating balls of light, sometimes bright enough to be visible during the daytime, and one woman who saw such lights experienced something else along with them.

"It felt like a cold hand on my elbow area," she said. "I could even feel the fingers. Not in a bad way . . . but it was just there. Then I heard a whisper in my ear that sounded like 'Let's go.' I couldn't tell if it was a boy or a girl, but my first thought was a younger boy. So I just went. I just went and the hand stayed on my elbow for about 20 minutes before I felt that part of my arm warm up again."

With history going back well over a century, I imagine that people other than David Smith and the young girl have died in floods, fire, and accidents at the Oaks and that their spirits haunt it as a result.

The Oaks is still up and running today and is open year-round. It is filled with thrill rides like the Disk O, Looping Thunder roller coaster, Rock 'O Plane, Screaming Eagle, Spider, and Zoom Coaster, and it has plenty of rides for youngsters as well, including the carousel, Big Pink Slide, bumper cars, Ferris wheel, Frog Hopper, and many more. During the winter months, people can roller-skate and take dance classes at the park. Whatever you do while you are there, keep an eye out for the children who remain, and for David Smith. I am sure they would appreciate a simple hello from you.

CHAPTER 9

Shanghai Tunnels
PORTLAND

WHETHER OR NOT YOU HAVE EVER BEEN to Portland, you may nonetheless have heard of the Shanghai Tunnels—and with good cause, as this underground maze is one of the most haunted locations in the world. The Shanghai Tunnels and the spirits that roam the dark and musty makeshift halls have been featured in countless documentaries and television shows like *Ghost Hunters* and *Ghost Adventures*. But, television aside, there have been thousands of reports by everyday people of paranormal activity in the tunnels, much of it captured in photographs and video and audio recordings. For many it is difficult to deny that the ghosts of shanghaied young men and ladies of the night still wander lost through the darkness of the dismal labyrinth.

The Shanghai Tunnels are exactly what their name suggests: a series of narrow passageways through basements of businesses on the ground above. These tunnels connect many businesses, including those that have long since been demolished, from Old Town Portland, into central downtown Portland, and finally to the waterfront area of the Willamette River.

Shanghaiing was a common but illegal practice in Portland in which strong, able-bodied young men and women were kidnapped and sold to waiting ship captains in search of unpaid laborers to perform physical work aboard their vessels. While shanghaiing was not exclusive to the Portland area, its tunnels were unique because of trap doors, also known as deadfalls, that were constructed and used to drop unsuspecting, often intoxicated individuals into the tunnels from businesses aboveground, where they were confined to makeshift cells until their services were bought.

Most who fell into the underground traps were young, unmarried men who had traveled to the area to work in the booming timber industry, transients, and others that no one would miss.

Shanghaiing became as lucrative a business, in fact, as the timber industry, and from 1850 to the early 1940s, Portland was known as either the Unheavenly City or the Forbidden City as a result of these illegal practices. Over the years, the tunnels became more than just a series of scattered cells to hold the unwilling, and during Prohibition saloons were constructed in the tunnels, along with drug dens where morphine was a common offering.

The victims of the Shanghai Tunnels were not exclusively men. Young women, mostly known prostitutes, were also kidnapped and held in cells to await the highest bidder. Many ships setting sail to the Orient needed attractive women aboard for housekeeping, cooking, and sexual favors. To this day, many will tell you that numerous spirits of such women wander the tunnels in search of an escape from the darkness.

It is estimated that more than 1,500 men and women were imprisoned in the tunnels every year and that several hundred of them died before being sold as slaves. Many suffered fatal injuries upon being dropped into the tunnels through the overhead trap doors, and others expired from health issues while being held captive. At one point in the late 1800s, at least 35 male prisoners died after drinking embalming fluid that was passed off as whiskey. Women became pregnant while in captivity and eventually lost their unborn children at the abusive hands of the businessmen and prospective buyers who frequented the tunnels. Some believe the walls here do talk, as the saying goes, and that they tell a violent and heart-wrenching story.

The name "Nina" is carved into a brick wall that was part of an elevator shaft for a hotel that once stood above the tunnels, and many believe Nina, who was sold into a life of prostitution, haunts the dark passageways today. She was one of many who sustained injuries after being dropped into the tunnels and later died from complications of those injuries. Many claim to have witnessed a full-bodied apparition that they believe to be Nina, and others say that Nina attempts to get the attention of those in the tunnels by tugging on their clothing.

There are other ghostly residents in the tunnels, albeit none as well known or as often seen as Nina, and people report male and female whispers, crying, moaning, and screams, as well as shadows and manifestations that there appear to be no explanation for.

You have a choice of a number of tours if you are interested in visiting the Shanghai Tunnels. Many visitors go into the tunnels on these excursions expecting long and winding passageways and many rooms and cells, but the tours go to only about half a dozen rooms. All tours run at least an hour and a half, however, and I feel the price is worth it for history buffs and those interested in the paranormal alike.

The Shanghai Tunnels Heritage Tour focuses primarily on the sordid history of shanghaiing and human trafficking in the Portland Underground and gives visitors an idea of what those who became the unwilling victims to these illegal practices must have endured. It starts at a restaurant called Hobo's.

The Shanghai Tunnels Ghost Tour explores the alleged haunted history of the tunnels in more detail. Rich with dramatic retellings of the alleged ghosts, their lives and deaths, you will hear such spine-tingling phrases as "You can almost feel her watching you now . . . can't you?" The period costumes of the tour guides also leave visitors feeling as though they have crossed that invisible line into the dark and impure past of the tunnels. The three or four times I have taken this tour, however, flash photography was not allowed, and on some tours no photography at all is allowed, nor is video; audio is out of the question due to the number of people on the tour and noise from the restaurant and busy streets above. But if you love history, and get that chill of excitement at the prospect of glimpsing the ghost of Nina or one of the many other ghosts that purportedly roam the dark passageways, the tour will not disappoint.

Another offering is the Shanghai Tunnels Ethnic History Tour, which explores the past of the Chinese and Japanese workers in the area and how they relate to the activities that occurred in the tunnels.

Finally, you can book a personal Shanghai Ghosting Tour for groups of at least 15 and as many as 30 people, which will provide a firsthand look at the areas both above and below the ground. This two-hour excursion begins above the tunnels at the Skidmore Fountain on SW Ankeny Street, itself an historic location that was dedicated September 22, 1888, in memory of Portland druggist Stephen G. Skidmore, who died in 1883 (the fountain was partially financed by Skidmore's will and is a well-known landmark near the Portland Saturday Market). The guides lead groups on a street-level tour of the haunted history of the Old North End of Portland, after which they take visitors underground at Hobo's restaurant.

You do not have to believe in ghosts to enjoy the Shanghai Tunnels, and the history of the tunnels and of the area overall is as fascinating and heartbreaking as the paranormal lore. It shows the lengths people went to—and still go to—to acquire free labor. Human trafficking is still a big enough problem in the Portland area to warrant a dedicated task force, and it is not so much a case of history repeating itself as it is one of history continuing.

But if it is a ghost you are hoping to experience, Shanghai Tunnels is as good a place as any to seek that chance. Be it the saddened Nina or someone else who has remained behind seeking escape, visitors stand a good chance of experiencing something paranormal. We can only imagine what was left behind and remained embedded within the shabby walls of the tunnels—the fear, the anger, the greed. And, perhaps, a frightened and lonely young prostitute who may be waiting for you to rescue her from the darkness.

CHAPTER 10

Stark Street
PORTLAND

WHEN AN ENTIRE STREET IS CONSIDERED to be inhabited by ghosts, you know that Portland lives up to its reputation as one of the most haunted cities in Oregon. It is not at all unusual, in fact, for visitors to capture ghostly anomalies as they take pictures along Stark Street.

Stark Street is what many consider an epicenter for paranormal activity. Surrounded by water, former flophouses, and cemeteries, it is ripe with history and ghosts of the past. Many a paranormal researcher has documented activity with electromagnetic field (EMF) meters, video equipment, and digital still cameras. And many people have detected haunted happenings with the naked eye or ear—wispy figures and dark shadows darting across the street and behind buildings, glowing orbs floating just above visitors' heads, and the sounds of footsteps and whispers following close behind them. . . . It does not take someone long to realize that they are not alone.

Stark Street is certainly not without its history. The Witches Castle (see page 70) is found here, not far from where Danford Balch stood on the platform of the Stark Street Ferry and murdered his son-in-law, Mortimer Stump, with a double-barreled shotgun. Lone Fir Cemetery (see page 41), the oldest cemetery in Portland, also lies near Stark Street and is filled with reports of hauntings.

Stark Street was also the thoroughfare used by many a funeral procession. Caskets and mourners were unloaded from the Stark Street Ferry and the caskets pushed into horse-drawn hearses that led processions slowly down the street. This was commonplace and, if energy lingers, Stark Street is sure to host paranormal activity from the funeral processions alone. Coupled with the numerous homicides and suicides and unexplained deaths—some that remain active in the Portland police's cold case files today—some of these victims may still be seeking justice or simply peace from a violent death.

A walk down Stark Street can prove noisy because of cars, restaurants and bars, and other pedestrians, or it can be eerily quiet and stagnant. It is on the quiet nights, when every little sound seems amplified, that many feel that they are accompanied by someone they cannot see and experience that overwhelming feeling of being watched and followed.

Stark Street was named after Oregon merchant and politician Benjamin Stark, who was born in New Orleans in 1820 and ended up in Portland in 1845 as the cargo supervisor of the vessel *Toulon* in charge of bringing goods to a Portland warehouse. In 1846 he purchased 640 acres of land in the local area for $390 cash, visiting it only occasionally as he continued his work as a merchant. Despite his absence from Portland while at sea, Stark became an early civic leader as well as leading the city's Freemason membership—an undeniable status symbol even today.

In 1850, when Stark returned from San Francisco to set up shop in Portland, he was met with news that his claim on the 640 acres of land had been challenged. Eventually a settlement was reached with the other stakeholders, and Stark received the title to a triangular section of property in Portland between the Willamette River, Stark Street, and Ankeny Street.

In 1852, Stark was admitted to the bar and became a member of the Oregon Territory House of Representatives. He also participated in the 1853 hostilities between settlers and American Indians during the Rogue River Wars. That same year he married his wife, Elizabeth. And after Oregon acquired statehood in 1859, Stark was elected to its House of Representatives the following year, representing Multnomah County as a Democrat.

When Oregon's junior senator Edward D. Baker was killed in action in the American Civil War in 1861, Stark replaced him and served until the latter part of 1862. He was an advocate for slavery and opposed the creation of publicly financed schools. He did not run in the election for a permanent replacement for his seat.

Stark became wealthy selling off plots of his land in what is now downtown Portland before taking his law practice to New London, Connecticut, where he died in 1898 at the age of 78.

In 1987 the Clyde Hotel was renamed the Ben Stark Hotel and remained that way until 2005, when it became the Ace Hotel, and east-to-west running Stark Street was also named in his honor. Many of the reports of apparitions there are that of an elderly man in period attire, so it stands to reason that Benjamin Stark is still walking the street that bears his name in his beloved Portland.

If, while walking down Stark Street on a chilly, spooky night, you find your stomach rumbling, consider popping into Mother's Bistro for some fine dining because these Stark Street restaurants also have their fair share of spirits and paranormal activity. Take notice of the fake flowers that rest upon a wooden cabinet, along with an apple for a woman who allegedly drank herself to death there decades ago. There are also stories that this establishment was once home to a Chinese boardinghouse, opium den, and illegal gambling hall. And, apparently, lingering spirits are to blame for a series of mechanical issues that have plagued the block, including flooding from water heaters bursting unexpectedly, a paper shredder bursting into flames, and files being misplaced and rearranged. Explainable? Sure. But is it likely that spirits are culpable? Not so much.

Many of the buildings along Stark Street hold at least a bit of sordid history. Portland itself was, at one time, a hotbed for illegal gambling, drug dens, and shanghaiing. Houses of ill repute were plentiful and flophouses were on every corner. And when an entire neighborhood has so much paranormal activity, how could it not spill over onto the streets on which the spirits walked during their lifetimes? I liken it to overfilling a balloon with air—eventually it will burst and the contents will escape.

I have walked Stark Street many times, usually during the daytime and usually in awe of the buildings and the history of Portland. But when my friends and I walked the street while researching this book, we were fortunate to luck into a quiet night. It wasn't long before that feeling of being followed developed. We didn't speak, just listened. We tried to walk quietly and be aware of our surroundings. The first time we stopped to admire a building, we all heard four distinct footsteps behind us. They approached, and then stopped seconds after we did, but when we turned no one was there.

We realized that some of the wispy figures that had been reported could be explained by car lights or ambient lighting reflecting off glass or water, casting a light shadow that bounced from one reflective surface to another. And the only orbs we photographed were obvious moisture from the slight mist and snowflakes. This is not to say that what we experienced debunks all photographic data out there—we were just not fortunate enough to document any ourselves.

A few people were on Stark Street for the same reasons we were and wanted to catch a glimpse of any of the many reported ghosts. In speaking with these people, I found that many believe Benjamin Stark himself paces the sidewalks of Stark Street at night. He is described as a tall man with a long white beard and a long overcoat, usually walking with his head bowed so that witnesses never see more than the beard.

"I have seen him twice in the past four years," an older pedestrian told me. "No doubt about it. He was there and then he was gone. We love our history here, and most of us know what Ben Stark looked like. Solid as you and I. No doubt about it, it was Ben Stark."

Another man told me, "Portland had a history in the 1800s and early 1900s of being a rich city, but really we were just a Wild West town with a few extra frills. We might've had the bling, but lots of people died down here. There were a lot of murders. If it were me, I'd be walking around looking for justice too!"

I asked him if he had seen Stark or any other ghost on his walks on Stark Street.

"I've heard more than I've seen," he said. "Like getting ready to turn the corner of a block and hearing two guys fighting and a gunshot—or what I thought was a gunshot. But there was no one there. And footsteps, a lot of footsteps, either walking behind me or running past me. To be honest, the first time it happened I ran home and hid. It scared me to death. But the more I thought about it, the more I wanted to see what was down there. I've seen shadows, things like that, but still waiting to see Ben!"

I didn't see Stark while I was there either. I saw a few shadows that I was able to explain, and no ghosts crossed my path that night. But I completely understood what the man I spoke with said and want to go back again to catch a glimpse of Stark.

While we did not see anything out of the ordinary that night, we all heard the footsteps following us that stopped when we stopped. Had I been alone I might have let it pass and chalked it up to the anticipation I felt when we arrived. When four people hear and describe the same thing, however, it leaves less room for debate.

Whether it is Benjamin Stark who strolls along Stark Street or some of the many men and women who died after being shanghaied into a life of free labor or the victims of one of the many murders of the past, we may never know. But there is defi-nitely a presence or two down there on Stark Street. People have experienced it, visually and aurally, and with the photographic data that exists, it is hard to deny.

So when you are in Portland, perhaps staying at one of the many haunted hotels and after having had dinner at one of the many haunted restaurants, consider taking an evening walk down Stark Street and soaking in some of Portland's beautiful history. There is a good chance you could run into Benjamin Stark himself.

CHAPTER 11

White Eagle Saloon
PORTLAND

THE WHITE EAGLE SALOON on Russell Street in Portland may not be big in stature, but it is a giant in legend and
reports of paranormal activity. For decades many have called it
one of the most haunted places in Portland, and to this day it
upholds that reputation. Psychics have homed in on violence and
death, and paranormal research teams have accumulated data to
substantiate those claims. Today the White Eagle Saloon is best
known for its nightly rock music shows, its 11 original and simple guestrooms, and the outdoor beer garden that is open during
warmer months. Bands such as ZZ Top and the Isley Brothers

played this rock venue in the beginning of their careers, all on the original corner stage and ceramic tiled floor.

Even today the White Eagle remains true to its century-old roots, décor, and ambience, giving visitors an accurate visual experience of early 20th century Portland. Walking through the doors seems to blur one's sense of the present and the past. Built in 1905 by Polish immigrants Barney Soboleski and William Hryszko, the White Eagle offered other Polish immigrants a recreational outlet after long days at work—games of pool or poker while smoking cigars and drinking. And with the proper connections and the right amount of money, immigrants could also follow the steps to an upstairs brothel or downstairs opium den. In the basement of the White Eagle Saloon was a tunnel that connected to the notorious underground network that led to the waterfront known as the Shanghai Tunnels. Thus the making of paranormal legends began at the White Eagle.

It was not long before the White Eagle Saloon had acquired quite a violent reputation. Trolleys stopped at Russell Street and practically left passengers at the front door with the conductor yelling out, "Next stop, bucket of blood!" It was a rightfully earned nickname, as violent brawls were commonplace in the White Eagle, many resulting in deaths. But still, day after day, men poured in by the dozens after the final work bell sounded—and it remained this way until Prohibition hit in 1916.

Prohibition brought some temporary but drastic changes to the White Eagle Saloon. The taps went dry, and it became a gathering place for local children to get ice cream cones and other treats. According to legend, however, those who wanted a stiff drink could still partake for a stiff price in the basement.

Once Prohibition was repealed in 1933, the White Eagle Saloon went back to its beginnings, though with a much calmer clientele. Now hardworking men played honest games of pool, poker, and shuffleboard while enjoying hearty meals and beer, while older men played rummy and smoked Irish cigars in the back room. They were in good spirits—and in the company of spirits of the past.

In the early, rougher days of the White Eagle Saloon, when the upstairs brothel was the most popular attraction, there were many reports of prostitutes beaten or even killed. The treatment of these ladies of the night was not humane by any standards. The brothel had two separate areas, one that housed white women and another that housed black and Chinese women. Not only were these women not allowed to keep any of the money they generated, they were forced to work off debts for room and board. According to reports, any unfortunate children born to these enslaved women were removed and disposed of immediately, in order to get the mothers back into "working condition."

One particular prostitute, Rose, was the favored working woman of the owner, and he considered her to be his personal property. But as has happened many times in such situations, a customer fell deeply in love with Rose and wanted to take her away from a life of prostitution. Rose feared repercussions from the proprietor should she leave the establishment, however, so she followed her head instead of her heart and sadly refused the young man's offer. Angered by the refusal, the young man confronted the owner and was nearly beaten to death. He was nonetheless undaunted and still very much in love with Rose, so he once more pleaded with her to leave the brothel and run away with him to be his wife—and, once more, Rose refused. Angered, the young man snapped and stabbed her to death in room 2.

There have been many reports over the years, both in room 2 and elsewhere throughout the building, from people who have heard a woman sobbing. Numerous people have reported seeing a full-bodied apparition of a young, attractive woman in her mid-20s in the halls of the former brothel. And some have even claimed to have been propositioned by a mist-like figure as they lay in bed in one of guest rooms. Could this be Rose or one of the many other former prostitutes who met their demise at the White Eagle Saloon? History tells the beginning of the story, but it is up to us to seek out the ending.

Another resident spirit, an orphan called Sam, was taken in by the owners as a child. He lived in and worked for the White Eagle Saloon for his entire life and eventually passed away in his room as an old man. For a number of years, Sam's belongings remained in his room just as he left them. On numerous occasions, however, his possessions were reported to have been moved to other rooms, despite claims from everyone working at the tavern that they had not moved them. And over the years, passersby have reported seeing a man looking down from second-floor windows as though he were observing them.

The White Eagle Saloon housekeeper, Crystal, has always had strange experiences as she prepares rooms for the next guest. She has completed rooms, left them, and upon her return found pillowcases removed from pillows and placed in other locations around the room. She has always felt that she was not alone in room 7, and it's a room that many are uncomfortable in. When I made a second trip to the White Eagle Saloon, I and my team members Laura Schier and Becky Kanipe asked Crystal if we could see it. She escorted us to the room, and the door opened without her using the key card. The room is always locked, so of course this intrigued us. The rooms are not big and stay true to their boardinghouse feel, along with shared bathrooms, but room 7 definitely gave us an odd feeling, as though we were being watched. As we left the room, I took a picture of the door and immediately noticed a slight purple light in front of it. With no light source to cause this effect, it definitely left me wondering what or who might be causing it.

The darkest secrets of the White Eagle Saloon are held for eternity within the walls of the basement. Black and Chinese women were brought in from the docks and shuffled through the tunnels of the basement, where they were held as prisoners until they were sold or impressed into prostitution. The spirits of these wronged and desperate women seem to clog the air within the basement, creating a heaviness that many can physically feel.

From the depths of the basement, a tunnel had been dug to assist men in drugging young male patrons and then selling them to ship captains who passed through the area via the Willamette River. This was called "shanghaiing," and the Shanghai Tunnel system has since become known as one of the most haunted places in the world. After a night of drinking and carousing, the men were drugged and transported to makeshift cells until a buyer was located. They never had a chance.

In more recent times, there was an office in the basement where managers and staff members worked in what they thought was a quiet and out-of-the-way area. At night, after the saloon closed and the patrons were home and asleep, some employees heard music coming from the saloon above them but upon investigation found nothing that could be the cause of the sounds. On another occasion, coins fell from the ceiling of the basement after one employee reported feeling what he described as a strong earthquake that seemed to shake the entire building. He immediately turned on the television, expecting to hear news of the quake, but there was nothing about it.

A former waitress reported that one night as she descended the stairs toward the basement office, in view of the owners, she was violently shoved from behind and fell the full length of the stairs. She sustained minor injuries and, upon returning to work, never went into the basement again.

The most popular area of the White Eagle Saloon is still the bar. It is a long and narrow area that stretches the length of the building from front to back. There is a corner stage and a small dance floor near the rear of the room. Men in period clothing have been reported sitting at the bar or striding across the dance

A ghost known as Sam is often seen and heard in this hallway of the White Eagle Saloon.

floor. The spirits have been known to frequent the restrooms as well, and customers have reported seeing apparitions of women standing behind them in the ladies' room mirrors. One female customer even reported that she became involved in a toilet paper fight over the stall walls one evening after a few drinks, but that after she exited the stall she saw that the one next to her was empty and open.

Based on the experiences of customers, it would seem that the guest rooms have the most frequent and intense paranormal activity. Some patrons have stayed on more than one occasion with no activity, but others have experienced things that shook them.

One couple reported that while staying in one of the saloon's guest rooms they awoke during the night to see a well-dressed,

White Eagle Saloon welcomes guests to wine, dine, and slumber with the spirits.

middle-aged man standing at the foot of their bed, looking at them with a blank stare. In the morning, they attempted to explain away the apparition as a dream but realized it would be almost impossible for both of them to dream the exact same thing. They have returned on a few other occasions, hoping to catch a glimpse of the specter to no avail, but they have since heard women's voices and men arguing in the hallways.

A guest in room 13 reported that her first stay at the White Eagle was also her last. During the night, she was awakened when the blankets were moved and pulled away from her shoulders.

"Even when I woke up they kept moving!" she told me. She spent the rest of the night on the floor with her coat draped over her. "I will come back to the bar, but I won't stay in the rooms again."

My personal experiences at the White Eagle Saloon and guest rooms were not quite as dramatic or intense as those described here, but they were certainly a bit out of the ordinary.

I don't drink, so bars are often an odd and uncomfortable place for me to find myself, but once fellow investigator Laura Schier and I ordered burgers, the feeling of being out of place quickly fell away. (I could write an entire chapter on the amazing food alone but will leave that to a restaurant critic.) The White Eagle was one of the first stops on our haunted road trip, and it was worth every mile we drove. Throughout the afternoon and well into the evening, we spoke to regular customers about their paranormal experiences at the saloon. Most had stories to tell, such as hearing voices, seeing glasses slide across tables, and catching fleeting glimpses of apparitions of those from bygone times.

As nighttime descended upon us, we made our way to one of the saloon's queen rooms, which was simple and tasteful, with shared bathrooms in the hall. We decided to stay awake as long as we could, planning our route for the next day, lest we miss something. During a lull in the conversation, we clearly heard footsteps across the room that seemed to stop in front of us. We waited quietly but heard no further movement. Deciding to get a few hours of sleep before the next leg of our journey, we said goodnight and lay down. Less than 10 minutes later, however, we both heard a soft female voice whisper "Goodnight." It wasn't frightening, nor did it unnerve us, but was instead rather calming and made us feel that whoever was there could hear us and acknowledge our presence.

Travelers passing through the Portland area should definitely put the White Eagle Saloon on their list of places to see. Visitors who want to spend the night can choose from bunk rooms that feature wood bunk beds, full rooms, or queen rooms, all with original porcelain sinks and shared bathrooms in the hall. Suffice it to say, the trip back in time is priceless!

CHAPTER 12

Witch's Castle
PORTLAND

FOLKLORE, LEGENDS, AND GHOST STORIES
abound regarding the Witch's Castle, and as with so many purportedly haunted locations in the Portland area, one must carefully sift through the lore in order to filter out the truths. Even then,
it is sometimes difficult to paint a completely accurate portrait,
and one is left with a dramatic narrative at best. But this is also
what makes traveling to haunted locations so intriguing. Visitors
are left to decide whether their own experiences and senses re-
flect paranormal activity. But what most ghost hunting travelers
do know is to expect the unexpected.

The Witch's Castle is a site that ghost stories are built around—a moss-covered, deteriorating, creepy-looking shell of a building. It is indeed an eerie site to stumble upon along the forest trails of Macleay Park, especially to anyone who has not been forewarned of its existence.

Anyone researching the Witch's Castle will not find much about it, and even historians and experts cannot seem to come to a unified conclusion on the true origins of the structure. Facts get muddled, and one must rely on the most logical and retold version of its history, which appears here.

There is more history regarding the land on which the structure sits than on the structure itself. The first thing visitors see at the beginning of the forest trails is an aged historical marker placed by the state of Oregon that reads:

Danford Balch Homesite. Near this site stood the cabin of Danford Balch, his wife Mary Jane, and their nine children, all 1847 emigrants from Ohio and Iowa. In 1850, Balch took out a 640-acre Donation Land Claim whose boundaries today would be Vaughn Street and St. Helens Road, Twenty-Second Avenue, Cornell Road, and Aspen Street. This Willamette Heights district was known as the "Old Balch Place." In 1859, Balch was convicted and hanged for shooting his son-in-law. His hanging, the first legal one in Portland, and the subsequent disposal of his land made news well into the 20th century.

This much of the story must be factual enough to warrant this marker. After 1850, accounts tend to become convoluted, but we can deduce a number of things.

In all likelihood, 640 acres was too much land for Balch to tend singlehandedly, and he most certainly needed assistance clearing it. The employer interview process as we know it today was not commonplace in 1850, so Balch filled the helper position with a transient worker from Vancouver by the name of Mortimer Stump. The two men worked side by side for more than 12 hours each day, months on end, making noticeable progress on the land. As a result of spending so much time together laboring and conversing, they became fast, close friends, and eventually Balch felt comfortable enough with Stump that he invited him to lodge in the Balch family cabin. Unbeknownst to Balch, however, this decision was the beginning of his end.

Young love is something we have read about throughout our lives, heard about in song, and probably experienced at some point during our younger years. It stands to reason that it would also infiltrate the Balch cabin. . . .

Accounts say that before long Mortimer Stump fell deeply in love with Balch's 15-year-old daughter, Anna. The relationship was kept secret for fear of angering Balch and his wife or damaging Balch and Stump's friendship and working relationship. For these reasons the affair consisted of secret meetings, letters, and knowing glances. But it wasn't long at all before Stump felt the gnawing need to be honest with his friend and employer and admitted his love for Anna, asking for her hand in marriage. Balch, however, not only denied Stump his daughter's hand in marriage, he also immediately fired his employee and warned him to stay away from Anna, sentiments that were angrily echoed by Mary Jane Balch. Threats of curses and murder were tossed about in anger as Stump was ordered off the property.

In keeping with this Romeo and Juliet love story, none of these things deterred Mortimer and Anna. If anything, they were even more adamant on marriage than before. Almost immediately after Stump's termination, they eloped and were married by a justice of the peace in Vancouver, British Columbia, Canada. Anna knew that she could not return home to her family, so she and Stump moved in with his parents in Portland, where they spoke of their future together and shared dreams of a large family.

Once Danford Balch learned of the elopement, he fell into a maddened depression. For days he did not eat or sleep, and he consumed large quantities of his home-brewed alcohol. His out-rage festered to a boiling point and, after a few days of drinking, he ventured into Portland, where he encountered the new Mr. and Mrs. Stump at a shop on Front Street. Strong personalities clashed, and a heated argument ensued. Balch and Stump flung fists and threats, a scene that concluded with Balch storming off in a rage to retrieve a shotgun from his home 45 minutes away, while Anna and Mortimer headed to the Stark Street Ferry.

Anna had just boarded the ferry when Balch approached, now armed, and followed her, pleading with her to come home and trying to convince her that she was not mature enough to make a decision as permanent as marriage. But Anna was having none of it. As Balch continued to plead his case to his daughter, Mortimer leapt forward from behind his wagon to intervene. Danford Balch raised his gun and fired into Mortimer Stump's face and neck, killing him gruesomely and immediately. Stump's own parents were among the horrified bystanders who witnessed the murder on November 8, 1858.

Danford Balch was arrested at once. He was housed for the winter in a rickety jail with little warmth or comfort, but the small facility was not very secure and Balch escaped soon after and fled to the comfort of his own home. There did not seem to be any sense of urgency to recapture the fugitive, and the sher-iff, a friend of Balch, was not at all convinced that he had acted outside his rights as an employer and loving father.

Summer rolled around, and eventually Balch was arrested once again as he ate breakfast at home. He was returned to jail, and this time guarded heavily until his trial, which began on August 17, 1859. Balch seemed to have resigned himself to his fate and did little to assist his defense, although he did claim that his wife, Mary Jane, had bewitched him into taking the life of the man who had robbed them of their daughter. It is most likely that from this one statement the legend of the Witch's Castle was born.

The trial lasted just four days, and the jury reached a verdict within a matter of minutes. It found Danford Balch guilty of murder and sentenced him to be hanged to death on October 17, 1859.

This marked the first legal hanging in Oregon, and the public clamored for the best seats in an almost celebratory atmosphere. They brought their children and pets to the outing, along with parasols and blankets spread out for the baskets of food and drink they brought for the day. Among the spectators were Balch's own daughter, Anna, along with her in-laws.

Today there is very little left of the Balch family name: Balch Creek and the little historical marker beneath the bridge . . . and the tragedy. Locals still speculate and whisper about the man that was hanged.

What is physically left in this area is Witch's Castle. It was not built by Danford Balch or his family and is, rather, an old,

This marker indicates the site where the home of the tragic Balch family was located, in the area around what is now known as the Witch's Castle.

decaying restroom and park ranger station that was built in the 1930s by the government. It existed in its original condition until the 1960s, when ongoing vandalism and a flood finally destroyed it. What is left is the eerie shell, roofless, covered with moss, clinging ivy, and graffiti. It has been called Witch's Castle for decades and has a reputation throughout the state of Oregon of being haunted. It is all that scary movies are made of—an odd, out-of-place structure, a bloody tale of former tenants, and the haunting of the land on which it resides.

One of the most accepted stories about the Witch's Castle is that of an ongoing ghostly feud on the Balch land that gives rise to wicked laughter, sinister whispers, screams of terror, and angry specters—phenomena that give many a hiker second thoughts about venturing down the trails after dark. Many have also claimed to see dark figures darting between the trees and behind the shrubbery and in and out of the old stone structure. There have been reports of bright, glowing lights encircling the building before disappearing into the woods and even a few reports of full-bodied apparitions of young women and children—but, with the rarity of family photographs in the mid-1800s, it is impossible to confirm whether or not any of the apparitions resemble members of the Balch family. People I spoke with who have experienced what they feel is paranormal activity at Witch's Castle, however, do not stray from their accounts, and I tend to believe them and that this consistency points to the spirits of the Balch family haunting their old homestead.

I can assure you that after dark each noise, whether it is the falling of a leaf, or the crack of a twig, is amplified around the Witch's Castle. So whether the old stone building is haunted or not, it is not the most comfortable place to be when the sun goes down. I didn't see a ghost during my visit, but that doesn't mean they do not reside there, just that I was not in the right place at the right time. And, as we all know, history never dies.

Willamette Valley

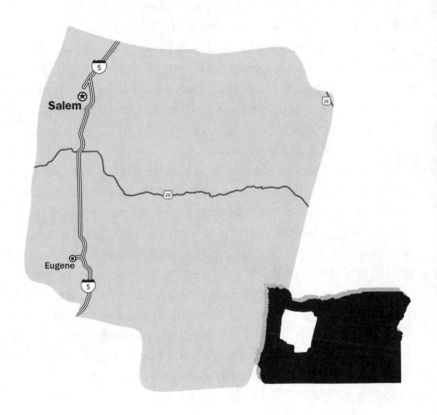

Salem
   Bush House Museum
   Elsinore Theatre

CHAPTER 13

Bush House Museum
SALEM

THE BUSH HOUSE MUSEUM is set apart from many similar museums in Oregon and is in a class of its own. Most historic homes that are now public museums have been refurbished, redesigned, or even rebuilt, but this is not the case with the Bush House Museum. For the most part, what visitors see today is what the Bush family saw day-to-day in the late 1800s and early 1900s—it is no re-creation of what might have been.

Nestled in Salem's historic district, the sprawling 100-acre estate is home to the original Bush house, the barn, the family's beloved greenhouse, a multitude of kaleidoscopic gardens, and sufficient pasturage for cattle. A simplified version of a Victorian Italianate–style home serves as the centerpiece. Victorian, when applied to architecture, refers to the style of homes during the reign of Queen Victoria, who ruled over Great Britain from 1837 until 1901, and the term Italianate refers to architecture inspired by Italian villas that became popular in the United States between 1850 and 1890. The combination of the two distinctive styles set the Bush home apart from most others in the area.

The interior of the Bush house is a combination of elegance and a sense of independence that is reflective of the family that occupied it. The twelve rooms that are open to the public are filled with charming original furniture, as well as what at the time were considered modern conveniences. A state-of-the-art central heating system was installed when the home was built in 1878, even though the home's 10 fireplaces, each meticulously carved from imported Italian marble, were more than enough to keep the house warm. Each of the upstairs bedrooms was equipped with marble-topped sinks and provided hot and cold running water via indoor plumbing. All of this was virtually unheard of—and unaffordable—in 1878.

Most of the wallpaper visitors see in the home today is also original and imported from France. Asahel Bush II lit his home using the innovative Tirrill's Gas Machine, and the gaslight fixtures in the home are the same ones that lit up dark nights more than a century ago (although some have been converted to electric for practicality). Inmates of the state penitentiary built the wood-burning kitchen stove in 1877, and it is still functional and used today. The superb craftsmanship of the walnut and mahogany staircases, rails, and bannisters have turned the heads of many an admirer of woodworking. This was the beauty and luxury with which the Bush family surrounded themselves for the next 75 years.

Asahel Bush II, an attorney, banker, 1892 delegate to the Democratic National Convention, and most notably, newspaper owner and publisher, is familiar to many Oregon historians. Everything that he aspired to do he did successfully.

Bush was born in Westfield, Massachusetts, in 1824. At age 17 he moved to New York and became an apprentice printer, and in 1850, at age 26, he passed the bar in his home state of Massachusetts and became a lawyer at an age when most young men were still sowing their wild oats. He arrived in Oregon later that year and settled in Oregon City, where he founded the *Oregon Statesman* newspaper. Then, in 1853, Salem became the territorial capitol, and Bush did not hesitate to pack up his newspaper and move it to the new political hub. The newspaper would later become the *Salem Statesman Journal* and is still going strong today as the *Statesman Journal.*

As the politically inclined editor of the *Oregon Statesman,* Bush gave a substantial voice to the Democratic Party through his publication. Despite being known as a racist and defender of slavery, Bush supported the Union during the Civil War and favored the prohibition of slavery in Oregon. He became the first official printer for the state of Oregon and held that honor until 1863, when he sold the newspaper and went into banking, opening the Ladd and Bush Bank in Salem with partner William S. Ladd. Many say he made this change in careers in response to the death of his wife, Eugenia, who passed away suddenly from tuberculosis; with banker's hours, he would be able to spend more time with his four young children, 6-year-old Estelle, 4-year-old Asahel III, 2-year-old Sally, and 1-year-old Eugenia. Bush appeared to be as proud of being a single father as he was of any of his lucrative careers.

After Bush bought out his partner's share of the Ladd and Bush Bank, it became the strongest financial institution in the entire Pacific Northwest. With this latest achievement, Bush decided it was time to settle in and build the house of his dreams for his family. With money being no concern, he moved the farmhouse he and his children had been living in for years to Mission Street and hired accomplished architect Wilbur Boothby to construct the stately Victorian Italianate mansion that sits there to this day.

The Bush children grew up privileged yet humble and did well in life as they grew older, making their father extremely proud. While they did not want for anything, they also did not flaunt their wealth and made friends from every walk of life. Estelle, Sally, and Asahel III graduated from college and entered adulthood with the same style and grace as their father. Estelle married soon after college, Asahel Bush III followed in his father's footsteps and entered into a career in banking, and Sally returned to the family home to live with her father, assuming management of the mansion.

Eugenia, however, did not fare as well. In 1880, while attending college in Massachusetts, she developed schizophrenia and returned home. The story gets a bit muddled at this point, and there are two accounts of Eugenia's fate.

The first version is that Asahel was so embarrassed by his daughter's mental condition that he could not bear the thought of her being seen in public and kept her hidden in the basement of the mansion. She was not held prisoner, nor was she kept in deplorable conditions, and many say she was well cared for and had the best of everything . . . except for freedom and the luxury of being outdoors.

Proponents of the other version of the story say that Eugenia was sent away to a mental institution in Boston that cared specifically for the wealthy where she received the best in psychiatric and medical care that the era had to offer, but that she did not return to the family home until after her father's death in 1913.

Unfortunately, no documentation conclusively substantiates either story. Either way, she is said to have lived in the Bush Mansion with her sister Sally until her death at the age of 70.

Four years after Asahel Bush II died, his children donated more than 50 acres on the east side of the property to the city of Salem for use as a park in honor and remembrance of their father and his legacy in the area. They also specified that when Sally and Asahel III passed away, the rest of the property, including the family mansion, would also go to the city of Salem.

All of the Bush children lived well into old age. Sally lived in the mansion and maintained the sprawling property until her death at the age of 76 in 1946. After the death of his sister, Asahel returned to the Bush Mansion in 1948 at the ripe old age of 90. Though mentally he was still a young man, age had slowed him physically, and he installed an elevator in the mansion that allowed him to more easily move about between floors. He kept up the home and grounds as best he could until his death in 1953 at the age of 95.

While there seems to be no mention of grandchildren of the elder Asahel Bush, genealogical records indicate that Asahel Bush III married Lulu Hughes and they had a son, Asahel IV, in 1887. Estelle Bush married Claude Thayer and they had one daughter, Eugenia, in 1897. There are many Bush grandchildren and great-grandchildren in the area today.

Since 1953, the Bush House has been operated quite successfully by the Salem Art Association and was opened to the public as an historic museum with daily tours and special events. The house was listed on the National Register of Historic Places in 1974.

In 1963, the barn on the property was destroyed in a fire and was rebuilt with great care. The Bush Barn Art Center now houses two contemporary galleries and one consignment and rental gallery and is also home to classrooms for community art classes and the always-popular pottery studio.

The conservatory that Asahel Bush built for his daughters in 1882 is now the oldest greenhouse in Oregon. It is filled with plants associated with the era in which the Bush family lived on the property and includes many rare and unusual varieties.

Each year during the third weekend in July, the Bush House property comes alive with the annual Salem Art Fair and Festival. Tented vendors line the property as live music and other forms of entertainment catch the eyes and ears of visitors. This unique event features more than 200 artists of all sorts and also includes two entertainment stages, beer and wine gardens, hundreds of vendors, food courts, and a kid's court that provides hours of education and fun with art activities for the whole family. Altogether, it is something that the Bush family would undoubtedly be pleased to see in their own backyard.

With all the music and art and laughter on the grounds, ghosts are probably not the first thing that would come to mind for most people. But throughout the more than six decades that the Bush House Museum has been open to the public, there have been countless reports of ghostly figures and phenomena.

Most believe that the ghosts are none other than the members of the Bush family themselves remaining in the place that brought them so much happiness in life. By all accounts it was the perfect life of the perfect family in a perfect town. And one might even be inclined to believe as much if it were not for the possible confinement of mentally ill Eugenia, who is what many consider the skeleton in the closet.

I have spoken with many who have either toured the home or worked as volunteers at the site, and most say they have not only heard and seen the ghosts of the Bush family, but have also seen things move right in front of them.

"It wasn't a drastic movement, not like things being thrown across the room," one woman told me. "But I did see a vase on a table in the living room slide about three inches across the table-top, and I heard it moving. I would have thought I was going a little crazy if my husband hadn't seen it too!"

Other people I spoke with said they have seen the shadowy figure of a man in a suit that looked to be fidgeting with a pocket watch on a chain.

The Bush House Museum still houses most of the Bush family's personal belongings.

"I never really knew what the senior Bush looked like until after the tour," another woman told me of this experience. "But when I looked up pictures online I knew in an instant that was who I saw."

Yet others have heard a young woman crying and sobbing breathlessly. Could this be Eugenia, tormented by the schizophrenia that changed and dictated her life? Many say that it is.

People have also reported seeing a woman looking out from one of the top-floor windows in the evenings and a mist-like figure floating between rooms. Visitors have heard whispers, both the often-reported crying and conversations that sounded as though they are coming from a room just around a corner. Such reports are too similar and too frequent to disregard.

Unfortunately, when I visited the Bush House Museum I did not experience anything paranormal, as much as I hoped that I would, but this in no way diminishes the relevance of what others have experienced. Ghosts are not performers and do not do tricks on command, and it is always a matter of being in the right place at precisely the right time. But even though I did not experience anything paranormal in the home, I did feel the history and was surrounded by the same things that the Bush family looked at, touched, and admired. I saw the work that went into each stairway bannister and rail, handcrafted 100-year-old furniture, and fixtures that looked as though they had just been taken off a showroom floor. I could imagine the pride the Bush's had for their home and their property, and that kind of happiness and love cannot die and remnants of it always persist.

The Bush House Museum is one place I hope you will visit when you are in Salem. It is so much more than just the mansion, and the grounds are filled with beauty and family fun. Pack a picnic lunch and enjoy the gardens, lush greenery, and fir trees. And don't forget to glance up at the upstairs window to see if one of the Bush daughters might be looking back at you.

CHAPTER 14

Elsinore Theatre
SALEM

OREGON, along with the rest of the world, is not at a loss for haunted theaters. Old theaters and ghosts, in fact, seem to go hand in hand, and this is certainly the case with the Elsinore Theatre in Salem.

The Elsinore Theatre opened its doors to an eagerly awaiting public on May 28, 1926, sitting smack dab in the middle of a lot that was once a livery stable. Theater owner George Guthrie envisioned a Tudor Gothic–style structure reminiscent of the castle of Elsinore where Shakespeare's play *Hamlet* is set, and that is exactly what he got from the able design firm of Lawrence and Holford. (One of the members of the design team, a man named Ellis Lawrence, became the founding dean of the School of Architecture at the University of Oregon.) It all came at a price, however, and while the Elsinore began with a budget of $100,000, its final cost exceeded $250,000, and rumors were rampant that Guthrie was on the verge of bankruptcy.

Guthrie's dreams became a reality with the opening of the Elsinore Theatre, and it quickly established a reputation as the finest, most elegant theater between Portland and San Francisco. The opening day show was the silent film *The Volga Boatman*, from the legendary Cecile B. DeMille, and it was musically accompanied by the selection *Finlandia* by Jean Sibelius on the theater's 900-pipe Wurlitzer organ.

A great number of memorable vaudeville performances, such as the twice-weekly act of Fanchon and Marco, graced the stage of the early Elsinore Theatre, as well as some promising newcomers to the Hollywood circuit, including Edgar Bergen and Charlie McCarthy, Clark Gable, and John Philip Sousa and the Marine Band. Theatergoers left with stars in their eyes and a swoon in their hearts.

A mere three years after Guthrie saw his dream of the Elsinore Theatre come to fruition he leased it to Fox West Coast Theatres. The talkies had just taken movie lovers by storm, and the theater company made all the necessary changes to accommodate the newest form of cinematic entertainment. One year later Guthrie leased the theater to yet another well-known name, Warner Brothers Theaters, which stayed in it for the long haul and ran the Elsinore until 1951.

Warner Brothers made the Elsinore a successful movie house for many years, and they added other attractions for the residents of Salem as well. One such popular weekly event during the 1930s was the auditions for Zollie's Mickey Mouse Club Matinee. Singers, dancers, and musicians came from miles around to take a shot at the local notoriety, and the very best were handpicked to perform on the Elsinore stage the following Saturday. The host was Zalmon Marcola "Zollie" Volchok, a local teenage celebrity, and the Mickey Mouse Club Matinee starred a regular group of young people, including a talented young trumpet player named "Doc" Severinsen, who later went on to fame on *The Tonight Show*. The audience, mostly children accompanied by their parents, enjoyed a show filled with live skits, cartoons, and music from the Wurlitzer. Even today some of Salem's oldest residents have their faded Mickey Mouse Club creed cards, the words etched into their memories:

I will be a square shooter in my home, in school, on the playground, wherever I may be. I will be truthful and honorable and strive to make myself a better and more useful citizen. I will respect my elders and help the aged, the helpless, and children smaller than myself. In short, I will be a good American.

If you walk the streets of Salem and see a smiling elderly person, there is a reasonable chance he or she was a Mickey Mouse Club member who became an upstanding and honorable citizen.

In 1954 the Elsinore Theatre once again changed hands and was sold to the Foreman Brothers. By this time the theater was in a steady decline from its once majestic status in Salem and had become a second-run movie house, falling victim to time, Mother Nature, and vandals. The once-beautiful stained glass windows in the upper lobby had been so badly damaged that they were boarded up, and the old Wurlitzer was broken down and sold for parts. The history of the Elsinore seemed to be dissolving and, in 1980, the theater was set to be demolished.

During the same year the grassroots organization Save the Elsinore Committee began to work with local authorities to save the theater from destruction. Eventually the theater was rescued from the wrecking ball, but the committee was not having as much luck with any other major changes. Two ballot measures, one for its purchase and much-needed restoration and another for operational funding, were defeated in 1981.

Eventually, the Save the Elsinore Committee obtained permission from the owner to use the theater for 18 days each year for a variety of free community events, in hopes of convincing the public of the need for the Elsinore and reversing its fate. These free public events drew some 75,000 people.

Until 1987, the Elsinore was one of only three active movie theaters in Salem with much of its clientele coming from Willamette University. The Elsinore had two attractive features that drew the college crowd—low admission prices and proximity to the university campus. But soon a brand new seven-screen theater opened only blocks away, and that ended the life of the Elsinore as a commercial movie theater.

In 1989, the Elsinore was sold to Act III Theaters with the stipulation that the community retain limited use of it. A year later Act III decided they had no use for the 60-year-old theater, and it once again was put up for sale. This time the Save the Elsinore Committee jumped at the opportunity to own the theater and immediately launched fundraisers to raise the purchase price. They accomplished their goal and became the proud owners of the Elsinore. The committee continued to raise funds for operational costs through the Salem community and by appearances from Hollywood celebrities that included Gregory Peck and James Earl Jones. In 2000, Peck presented the final performance of his highly popular touring show, *A Conversation with Gregory Peck*, on February 20 on the stage of the Elsinore Theatre. He closed the performance with these words:

I just want to say you have to do great things with a theater like this. I am so impressed. It's quite possibly the outstanding venue on our tour. I am most enthusiastic about the possibilities of this theater and I hope you will lend your strongest support.

The Elsinore Theatre was placed on the National Register of Historic Places in 1994. It is now a nonprofit organization with the following mission statement: "Promote, protect, and enhance the Elsinore as an historic national landmark and performing arts center."

With such a shaky history, and coming so close to demolition, it is no wonder that ghosts are said to remain at the Elsinore. One might expect that even they continue to fight for the theater they loved so much in life. These ghosts are many, both male and female. According to many who have witnessed the strange goings-on at the theater, the ghosts seem to be most attracted to live performances, and it is quite possible they have been there since the vaudeville days.

There is what people call the "legendary cold spot" on the stage, so cold that it raises the hair on one's arms and neck. People have also reported mistlike figures in the scaffolding above the stage, as well as the figure of a man in a suit walking into the theater—not walking down the aisles but, rather, right through the seating. And those who work at the Elsinore report the strong feeling of someone sitting or standing close by their sides when no one is there. The general consensus of those who spend a great deal of time at the theater is that former actors, directors, stagehands, and other personnel remain at the Elsinore.

A few specific ghosts linger within the theater walls. Numerous psychics have identified a male spirit as that of George Guthrie himself, believing him to still be enchanted with his castle-like theater and to continue overseeing productions on the stage he built.

It is also said that back in the 1930s a young boy was murdered in the restroom and that the killer was never identified or apprehended. Over the years, a handful of witnesses have reported seeing blood appear on the floor, walls, and mirror, and then disappear quickly, as though it were a glimpse into the past. And while my research has not revealed any reports of a full-bodied apparition of the boy, I have heard reports of a shadowy figure, smaller in stature, that is seen most often through the reflection in the

Elsinore Theater is still as grandiose as the day it was built.

mirror, darting quickly back and forth across the room. A boy has also been heard crying, moaning, and whispering "Mama."

Another often-told story is that original owner George Guthrie's daughter fell to her death at the theater and that her spirit remains in the area where she died. There are many accounts of a young woman who is seen in the upper balcony, simply standing and staring at the stage. She is also seen, usually as a semi-transparent figure in white, pacing back and forth in the front of the balcony.

When I visited the Elsinore, I immediately felt overwhelmed by many presences. I am not a psychic or a medium, but nonetheless I felt surrounded by people I could not see. It was not an unpleasant feeling, but it was surprising that it was so noticeable.

I also felt many cold spots without ever going onto the stage and found myself whispering to my friends, "Did you feel that? Did you hear that? Did you see that?" There was no fear in those questions, but there was lots of excitement.

"Can you see me?" I heard a distant voice ask as we were leaving the theater. I stopped immediately and looked around the lobby, hoping that I could see the person who asked the question. "I wish I could," was, however, all I could reply with.

"If these walls could talk," is an old saying I heard many times while I was growing up. The Elsinore Theatre reminded me that walls can indeed talk, that they have a story to tell, that they have people to introduce you to, and that they have a history that begs to be remembered. The walls of the Elsinore can talk, and they spoke loudly and clearly. And if I could speak for them I would say, "Here I am. I am the underdog. They wanted to break my bricks and shatter my glass, but I am still standing. I am old but strong in heart, and I still have much to offer. I promise to make you smile."

And I smiled as I left the Elsinore. It is a location I will never forget, and when people ask me if the theater is haunted, I reply with an emphatic "Yes!" It has so many ghosts that they feel like members of the crowd. They are there for the same reason anyone goes to the theater: to enjoy a majestic, historic Salem landmark. And maybe a good movie too.

Oregon Coast

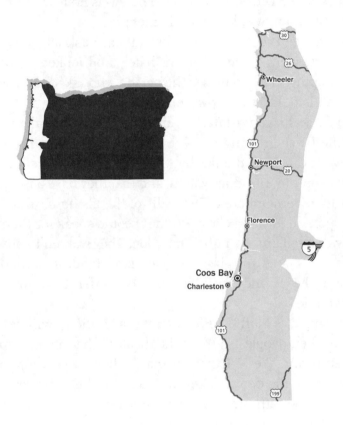

Charleston
World War II Lookout Bunker

Coos Bay
Marshfield Pioneer Cemetery

Florence
Heceta Head Lighthouse

Newport
Yaquina Bay Lighthouse

Wheeler
Old Wheeler Hotel

CHAPTER 15

Heceta Head Lighthouse
FLORENCE

OVER THE DECADES, the mere utterance of the name Heceta Head Lighthouse has become synonymous with the words *haunted* and *ghost*. Rarely do you hear the name mentioned without the addition of one of the previous words attached. But this is a day and age when the word *haunted* will bring visitors across the country to check into this majestic bed-and-breakfast for the chance to witness a specter with their own eyes. And this is the case with Heceta Head Lighthouse.

Many readers may be familiar with Heceta Head Lighthouse without ever having been there, as it has been featured on
numerous television shows and documentaries, including *Legendary Lighthouses* on PBS, another short documentary on Oregon Public Broadcasting called simply *Heceta Head Lighthouse*,
and a number of paranormal reality television shows. It is also
the subject of countless books focusing on either its historical or
paranormal aspect and often a mix of both.

Heceta Head Lighthouse is located in what is called the
Devil's Elbow, 13 miles north of Florence, Oregon, and 13 miles
south of Yachats, Oregon, at Heceta Head Lighthouse State Scenic Viewpoint. It keeps watch over sailors from 150 feet up a
205-foot headland, from which it provides a breathtaking view of
the Pacific Ocean. It was built in 1894 and named for Spanish
Explorer Bruno Heceta, a Spanish Basque explorer of the Pacific
Northwest who was born in 1744 in Bilbao, Spain.

Amidst reports that Russian settlers were in Alta, California,
Antonio Maria Bucareli y Ursua sent Heceta to Alta to either
confirm or quash such rumors. Aboard the vessel *Santiago* and
accompanied by the schooner *Sonora* and a 16-man crew, Heceta
embarked on a recon and mapping mission to Alta, California,
and the Pacific Northwest and became the first European to see
the mouth of the Columbia River. On July 30, 1775, *Santiago* and
Sonora parted ways. *Santiago* continued on to what we now know
as the border between Washington state and Canada, while
Sonora sailed up the coast, eventually reaching and entering the
Sitka Sound near what is now Sitka, Alaska. Heceta cut his trip
short because of an outbreak of scurvy, but not before making
note of the headland that now bears his name.

Prior to Heceta's arrival in the area, Heceta Head was used
for fishing and hunting by the American Indian tribes who populated the area, most notably the Siuslaw tribe, which resided in
the sand dunes just south of the promontory's rocky cliffs.

Construction of the Heceta Head Lighthouse began in 1892. It was built with lumber from local mills, cement from San Francisco, and rock quarried from the Clackamas River for the base of the tower. Laborers worked grueling 10-hour days in all kinds of weather at a rate of $2 per day, and even the highest-paid carpenter received only $4 a day. Other buildings associated with the lighthouse—the lighthouse keeper's quarters, the barn, the oil house—were completed in a timely fashion in January of 1893. But the lighthouse tower required more excavation work, and it was not completed until August of 1893. The lamp and its lens, which contained eight panels and more than 640 prisms, took more time to complete and assemble. Heceta Head's guiding beacon shone brightly for the first time on March 30, 1894. The light is still the most powerful on the Oregon coast and can be seen from more than 21 miles out to sea.

Visitors are told, sometimes tongue in cheek, that the lighthouse tower itself is not haunted. In fact, I spoke with volunteers who, despite having experiences in or around the lighthouse tower, have been told to "never say the word *haunted*" in relation to the tower. But the strange and unexplained occurrences in the light keeper's house at Heceta Head have led to it being called one of the 10 most haunted houses in the United States. For more than six decades, residents of the light keeper's house and guests of the bed-and-breakfast have spoken of unusual incidents. But don't let the ghosts scare you away. Rue, the most well-known spirit, is always pleasant and seems to have a penchant for cleaning. She does not evoke fear in guests, and they generally enjoy her company after the initial shock of realizing they are seeing a ghost.

It is said that Rue was the wife of light keeper Frank DeRoy in the 1890s. Some claim that Rue bore a daughter during her time at Heceta Head, and that the girl drowned at a very early age after slipping from the dangerously high cliffs on the hill on which the light keeper's house sits, while others say she drowned in a nearby estuary. Yet others say there was no daughter at all, and if Rue was indeed the wife of DeRoy, no records or documents exist to verify either the marriage or a child from such a union. This does not mean there was no marriage or a daughter, simply that records of marriage or a birth cannot be found to validate the claims. This is not as unusual as it may sound—the paper trail sometimes disintegrates with the passage of time.

Some also say a cement slab somewhere between the lighthouse and the light keeper's house marks the grave of the child, but the location of any such marker is unknown and its existence unverified. Again, however, this does not mean that the marker does not exist—if it does, it is likely buried beneath a century of overgrowth.

After hearing of my team's investigation of Heceta Head Lighthouse, I cannot count the number of times I have been asked if it is haunted. And Heceta Head is the one location where I do not use the word *haunted*—it is, rather, apparently occupied by the spirits of a lovely lady and a few outspoken men. My personal encounters with Rue were friendly, sometimes mischievous. I still listen to the electronic voice phenomena (EVP) recordings of a woman's voice asking "Who are you?" and "Who's there?" and "Take me to the water." And the recordings of a man proudly stating his name, "My name is Frank Cole." And while the Oregon Parks and Recreation Department emphatically denies that the lighthouse tower itself is haunted, my experiences suggests otherwise. After climbing 150 feet up the trail to the lighthouse tower, I recorded the voice of an older man who said with a laugh, "You are not alone here."

Picturing that hike in my mind's eye, I recall the almost spiritual awe I felt standing at the base of the lighthouse tower, parts of it constructed from rocks that had been quarried only a few miles away. I thought of the workers who toiled through blood, sweat, and tears for a few dollars a day. Then, opening my eyes to the view of the Pacific Ocean on a clear, starry night was almost surreal. Sometimes one can only imagine that level of beauty and tranquility.

We snapped numerous still shots of the lighthouse tower that night, every side, every angle. But it was not until I returned home the next day and looked closely at the photographs that I saw the bearded face of an older man wearing what looked like a dark-colored captain's hat looking down at me from the window a hundred feet above. Had it been just one picture I might not have thought about it twice. But it was three pictures, each taken from a different angle, and in each picture his head seemed to turn and follow me as I made my way around the lighthouse with my camera. As I looked at these pictures, I wondered if this may have been the man I heard on my voice recorder telling me that I was "not alone here."

Heceta Head is now a popular bed-and-breakfast that offers turn-of-the-century-style rooms at reasonable prices.

The Mariner I and Mariner II Rooms both have a southern view of the Pacific Ocean and, decorated with nautical themes and handmade quilts, offer a restful night indeed.

The always popular Light Keeper's Room boasts an amazing view of the lighthouse and a private claw-foot bathtub.

Victoria's Room is the one in which the light keepers slept. Decorated with Victorian-era relics that take visitors back in time, it also has a more modern private bathroom with a marble shower that was constructed from an old closet. It provides peaceful slumber in the extra-high, four-poster bed—and maybe even a visit from Rue.

The Cape Cove Room is the lighthouse's coziest room and overlooks the historic Cape Creek Bridge, designed by Conde McCullough, one of America's most talented and well-known architects. White walls and linens make this room a calming experience.

The Queen Anne Room is fit for a queen and is the most romantic room in the bed-and-breakfast. Guests have a beautiful view of the forest and the gardens and can soak in a porcelain claw-foot bathtub and gaze at the beach below.

After a good night's rest, or a night spent visiting with Rue, guests will head downstairs to the dining room for a full seven-course breakfast. The menu changes with the seasons, but visitors will enjoy fresh herbs and produce picked right from the light station garden and the finest Oregon has to offer, including artisan cheeses, sausages, produce, and pastries. And if you are staying more than one night, you will be treated to a different breakfast each morning.

So if you are of the adventurous state of mind and would like to take a brief step back in time, Heceta Head Lighthouse might well be the place to escape to on your next vacation. It is history, it is home, and you are treated like family. Even by the ghosts.

CHAPTER 16

Marshfield Pioneer Cemetery

Coos Bay

BEFORE VISITORS SEE Marshfield Pioneer Cemetery, they first notice Marshfield High School, as both places share the same property and parking lot and are separated only by an old chain-link fence and gate. It is an odd sight during the day, when more than 1,000 students pass nonchalantly by the old cemetery, laughing and talking, when mere feet away those who built Marshfield, later known as Coos Bay, rest in eternal silence. But when the sun sets, the activity is not coming from the high school—it is coming from inside the chain-link fence.

Marshfield Pioneer Cemetery was established in 1891 by the Independent Order of Odd Fellows and is listed on the National Register of Historic Places. The IOOF purchased the eight acres of hillside property in Marshfield for $350 from local businessman

Charles H. Merchant. Each active member of the IOOF received one plot for himself, and the remainder was sold to residents of Marshfield. These plots sold quickly. The first burial is not known, as interments had been received since 1888 and sadly, no records were kept; the first official burial was recorded in 1891. It is disconcerting that for three years those buried will forever remain unknown. At some point a landslide occurred at Marshfield Pioneer Cemetery, and many of the unearthed bodies were relocated to more recently opened Sunset Cemetery, 3 miles south of town, something else that has helped obscure who is or is not currently buried where.

In 1906 the Odd Fellows Cemetery Corporation sold four acres adjacent to the Coos Bay (Marshfield) School District #9 for the tidy sum of $12,000, and immediate construction began on Marshfield's first public high school. Then, in 1914, the cemetery corporation opened Sunset Cemetery along Beaver Slough.

Today the appearance of Marshfield Pioneer Cemetery is generally acceptable, but this has not always been the case. For many years it was in such disrepair that had it not been for the tall, ornate headstones and crypts one may not have even been able to see it. Blackberry vines and other invasive species covered graves and headstones like an encroaching blanket. Vandalism was rampant with broken headstones, graffiti, and disrespect; as you maneuvered the overgrown walkways, you had to be cautious to avoid syringes, condoms, broken glass, and other dangerous objects hidden among trash that had been carelessly tossed onto the grounds. My team spent many hours trying to clean up the site and give back the dignity to those who interred there, working from sunup to sundown. But without support or assistance from those in charge of the cemetery, we knew we were fighting a losing battle. Eventually, a few years later, those responsible for the site decided to clean up the cemetery, and it is now at least satisfactory in condition.

Many believe that the cemetery is vandalized because it shares its grounds with the high school. What most do not know is that the Marshfield High School students give the cemetery the respect it deserves and have volunteered their time to locating long-missing headstone markers, cleaning the cemetery, and preserving its legacy. They have essentially adopted the cemetery, keeping it as clean as they can while researching its history. Not all Marshfield High School students are involved in these efforts or are this respectful, but I am thankful for those who are because I have ancestors residing in Marshfield Pioneer Cemetery.

My team's visits to Marshfield Pioneer Cemetery have not always been investigative ones, as members of PSI of Oregon are history buffs first and paranormal researchers second; without the history there could never be the paranormal. Many of our visits are to admire a time long gone and pay respects to those who helped build our small city, to pick up trash, and simply to surround ourselves with beauty and peace, corny as that may sound. The view of Coos Bay from atop Marshfield Pioneer Cemetery is spectacular, especially as the sun goes down. One can see the downtown area, the bay, and the incoming and outgoing ships, and watch the moon rise over the water. In fact, with many photographers on our team, most of our photos are not paranormal, but capture scenic beauty and the craftsmanship of headstones and obelisks from a century earlier. Not that we have not experienced paranormal activity at the cemetery, because we most assuredly have on many occasions.

The cemetery itself is not a large one. It spans just over half of a city block at the corner of Ingersoll Avenue and South Seventh Street. Its entrance is in the Marshfield High School parking lot. The east and west sides are supported by a tall rock wall, and the cemetery is separated from the school by an old chain-link fence. The gate is locked, and visitors must go to Coos Bay City Hall to retrieve the key. You must show a valid form of identification and pay a refundable key deposit of $5. It may seem like a lot to go through just to visit a cemetery, but vandals have forced this action and it is well worth the 20 minutes it takes to drive to get the key.

History buffs who visit Marshfield Pioneer Cemetery will be able to look upon the graves of veterans who served and died a century ago.

Morton Tower, for example, lived from 1840 to 1914 and was a Massachusetts volunteer during the Civil War. Wounded during the battles of Fredericksburg and Bull Run, he was captured and imprisoned by Confederate soldiers during the battle of Gettysburg. He was 1 of only 53 who escaped the confines of Libby Prison in Richmond, Virginia, and reached the safety of a Union camp. He moved to nearby Empire City in 1874 due to health reasons and died there in 1914.

Thomas Hirst lived from 1835 to 1903 and is credited with naming Sunset Beach State Park in Charleston, Oregon, and Gold and Silver Falls State Park in Coos Bay, both local landmarks.

Thomas G. Owen lived from 1845 to 1891 and served as a lieutenant in the 8th Missouri Cavalry for the Confederate States. He moved to Marshfield in 1873 and started the *Coos Bay News*, the first weekly newspaper in Coos County. He was also a Coos County sheriff.

Marshfield also has unmarked graves for those who lost their lives in 1910 when the steamship *Czarina* was grounded near the North Spit during bad weather and treacherous seas. They were just out of reach of any rescue service at the time but within full view of people in Marshfield and Empire City. For more than a day, onlookers gazed helplessly at the men on board who clung desperately to the ship's rigging, each eventually letting go and drowning due to exhaustion. In the end, just one person survived, and bodies washed ashore for weeks afterward. Today, *Czarina* remains one of the most tragic shipwrecks of the

Pacific Northwest. Many crew members came aboard the steamships for sporadic work and were not documented as employees. This made identification of many near to impossible. Six of the vessel's crew members who have never been positively identified are buried in a small, unmarked corner of the cemetery.

There are many tales of tragedy, murder, and historic figures who are interred at Marshfield Pioneer Cemetery. It is no wonder that a location so ripe with history and both famous and infamous individuals would also be ripe with paranormal activity. They have been ignored, disrespected, and hidden beneath decades of brush and brambles, but it seems now that they want to speak.

PSI of Oregon visited the cemetery one evening specifically to get shots of a full moon as it rose over the city below. Each team member repeatedly saw the apparition of a young woman dressed in late-19th-century attire and holding an infant. We captured one distant photo of the woman, but the EVPs revealed the most concrete data. Using a real-time digital voice recorder, we could hear her as she spoke and were able to respond instantly.

"We caught the sickness. . . . Please help my baby. . . ." we heard her say over and over. We also picked up terms such as "dropsy" and "the fever."

Later on in the year we were able to view the handwritten death records for many who had lived in Marshfield. We found many of the terms captured in our EVP recordings in these large books. We also found many drownings, shootings, and even a "death by ax." All of these records indicate the original burial site as Marshfield Pioneer Cemetery, but because there are so many unmarked and unknown graves at the cemetery, it is almost impossible to find those listed in the ledgers.

What I do know, however, is at least one young woman and her child still seek help from the living. While we cannot give her the help she is asking for, we can speak with her and

Marshfield Pioneer Cemetery was established by the Independent Order of Odd Fellows.

acknowledge her presence. And this small action is what most spirits crave—just to be acknowledged.

Whether you are seeking ghosts or history, you cannot go wrong with a visit to Marshfield Pioneer Cemetery. From the Civil War through World War I and World War II, military history is abundant, and from murder to suicide to the victims of shipwrecks, somber history is also abundant. But, in many ways, it is the history itself that keeps the cemetery alive.

If you decide to visit Marshfield Pioneer Cemetery, please acknowledge those behind the veil who still walk there and thank them for opening their doors to you. You may be surprised at the responses you receive.

Old Wheeler Hotel
WHEELER

HAUNTED HOTELS ARE NOTHING out of the ordinary in Oregon. In fact, the majority of hotels laid claim to spirits of one type or another. But few stand out in the way that the Old Wheeler Hotel does, from its history to its ghostly tenants.

Built in 1920, the Old Wheeler Hotel replaced two other wooden structures that had occupied the site. Originally called the Rector Hotel, it came along during a thriving economy and prospered in the little town of Wheeler, Oregon. One reason for the boom in the local area was the 1911 completion of a railway between Portland and Wheeler, enabling wood products from Wheeler mills to be transported easily to Portland for sale.

Wheeler remained well off until the early 1930s and the arrival of the Great Depression. And if that alone were not enough to bring the town to its knees financially, in the summer of 1933 the first of many large forest fires engulfed the timber surrounding Wheeler and devastated the basis of its economy. These fires, and this time in Wheeler history, are known as the Tillamook Burn and forever changed the community and its people.

The hotel was on a rapid decline from which it would never fully recover. Eventually, the establishment closed its doors and was purchased in 1940 by Dr. Harvey Rinehart, who turned the hotel into the Rinehart Clinic, an arthritis treatment facility. The upper floor of the former hotel served as rooms for patients receiving treatment for arthritis, and the bottom floor and basement served as areas for personalized treatment and physical therapy. The Rinehart Clinic would later expand to offer a wide variety of medical services and treatment before closing its doors in 1980. Dr. Rinehart's grandson, Harry Rinehart, has carried on his grandfather's legacy and practices family and general medicine in Wheeler.

The building changed hands many times over the years before falling under the care of Katie Brown and Greg Nichols. As they renovated and redecorated it, they soon became aware of the ghostly tenants who occupied the hotel along with them. Sounds of an antique Victrola would sometimes fill the lobby, or one of them would feel a ghostly hand on his or her shoulder. But Brown and Nichols did not flee the hotel. Instead, they welcomed their "guests" and tried to make them feel at home.

When my paranormal research team visited the Old Wheeler Hotel, we occupied three separate rooms and had access to the basement. One room in particular—room 3—seemed to have a static tingle to the air, and we concurred that we would focus mostly on that feeling and location, while other team members explored the concrete basement, which was once the treatment area of the arthritis clinic.

No lighting was available in the basement, so we walked carefully through the large area, even finding a "stairway to nowhere" that was apparently a remnant from the days as a medical clinic, when it had been a shortcut for transporting patients from their rooms to the treatment area. Digital cameras and voice recorders in hand, we asked questions, snapped pictures, and discussed the history of the hotel.

We then set up cameras and voice recorders in the hallways on the second floor and, as a last-minute decision, set up an old Hi8 video camera in room 3 before turning in for what remained of the night.

After returning home from a tiring trip with little sleep, we were stunned to see the video footage of room 3, and what was obviously a young boy running back and forth in front of the television that had been left on during the night. Not only did this apparition run back and forth, he also returned to stand directly in front of the television, as though whatever it was that was being broadcast drew his attention.

As we further reviewed the data we collected, we also heard voices and a squeaky-wheeled cart in the hallways on the second floor, and pained screams and a child's voice calling "Mommy" from the basement area. Despite the screams, we did not take this as anything untoward; we knew the history of the arthritis clinic and medical clinic, so screams of pain would not have been uncommon.

The trip to Wheeler, Oregon, and Old Wheeler Hotel will forever remain a favorite to me, and I left without doubt that the spirits who still reside in the rooms are friendly, intelligent, and as curious about us as we are about them.

The Old Wheeler Hotel is located at 495 North US 101 in Wheeler, Oregon. The view from the majority of the rooms is tranquil and serene, and it is not at all uncommon to see eagles and herds of majestic elk in the landscape, or the herons that land and fish on Nehalem Bay. For adventurers, there is fishing and kayaking on the bay, and visitors can even rent a boat at the marina across the street from the hotel and spend a day on the bay or cruise up the Pacific Ocean. And for the not-so-adventurous types, Wheeler has plenty of unique shops, antique stores, art galleries, gift shops, and a general store that seems to take you back in time with its wooden floors and quaint displays.

Or you may just want to stay in the hotel and visit with the spirits who reside there and with other physical remnants of the past. The lobby is filled with period items, including telephones, record players, and photographs. It is enough to keep anyone with a passion for Oregon history occupied for hours! And you don't need to worry about parking, because in this town of just 350, everywhere is within walking distance.

If you decide to visit Wheeler and spend the night at the Old Wheeler Hotel, ask for room 3. You will not be disappointed.

CHAPTER 18

World War II Lookout Bunker
CHARLESTON

ONE OF THE REMAINING World War II lookout bunkers along the Oregon coast sits halfway atop a Shore Acres State Park trail on Cape Arago Highway. Across from the former home of timber magnate Louis Simpson, this area is filled with hiking paths for all levels of experience. Fortunately for me, the trail that leads to the bunker is moderate, and most can manage the uphill hike with little to no experience.

This World War II lookout bunker is nestled among Douglas fir and pine trees about a third of a mile into the trail. During the war, the old cement structure was just one link in a solid chain of lookout posts that were constructed to guard the

Oregon coastline against enemy invasion. Time has taken its toll on this old building, but it still stands tall within the forest. Its roof is gone, but the walls and tall radar housings—which many people mistake for smokestacks—remain steadfast and almost majestic. The three rooms that make up the bunker are marred by graffiti and, often, the remnants of a night's party. While the trees have had 80 years to grow and block the view of the horizon, it is easier than you may think to stand atop the bunker and imagine seeing the brilliant blue sea before you and experience what it must have felt like to know you were protecting your own hometown during a time of great crisis.

The southern Oregon coast is still home to many World War II veterans and their families, and children and grandchildren have grown up listening to war stories and, on occasion, ghost stories. Stories change, of course, when they are passed from generation to generation and shared with others, but the core of a tale usually remains the same. Ghost stories about the World War II lookout bunker are among those that have survived the generations, and it is not uncommon to run into fellow hikers on this trail who are also there to investigate them.

One particular hiker I encountered and spoke with explained that this was his third visit in as many weeks after he had an odd experience in the bunker. My curiosity was piqued and I gently urged him to share his experience with me. With a handshake, he introduced himself only as Don and his dog as Keno. Don explained in an almost hushed voice that his first visit there was uneventful until he was packing up to leave. As he heaved his backpack onto his shoulders, he heard a deep voice near his ear whisper "It's safe."

This was Don's first experience with anything resembling the paranormal, so his departure that day was hurried. His subsequent visit a week later was similar. The surroundings were quiet as he waited—almost hoped—for another experience. Giving up after a few hours, he again prepared to leave and heard a voice similar to that which he had previously heard. "Stand down, man," the voice, once again near his ear, said. Don said at that point he sat back down and quietly sang "The Star-Spangled Banner."

"I am sure that anyone near me would've thought I was crazy," he explained. "But it was all I could think of to do. What do you say to someone you can't see?" I assured him I did not think he was crazy and found how he had responded to be respectful to our soldiers. He wished me luck on my visit and started down the hill with an over-the-shoulder wave. I haven't seen Don since but have no doubt that we will run into each other again.

As with many historic sites, locals continue to whisper that spirits of soldiers may still be in the bunker, protecting our country and keeping watch along its shores. I have visited this location many times during my life here on the Oregon coast—mostly out of respect for all that was given and lost during World War II—but it was not until 20 years into my research of the paranormal that I began to truly experience what many locals have said about its ghosts. So I loaded up a backpack with water and basic paranormal research equipment—my voice recorder, a digital camera, and a video camera—and took the hike once again with family and friends. This was not a formal investigation by any means, but what I came away with that day made me regard the bunker in a very different way.

The hike is entirely uphill and, at the top and to one side is the entryway for the bunker. The first room is approximately 20 feet by 20 feet. Beyond this chamber and through an opening whose door is long gone is a second room, which is the same size as the first. We speculated that this area most likely housed bunks, deducing that from the way the bolts in the walls were evenly spaced and stacked. Another doorless entry leads into the third room of equal size, next to which is a small opening the size of a dog door, as well as two openings that provide a view up into the towering radar housings. The final doorway leads outside to a trail that goes to the top of the bunker and ends next to the three radar housings.

As I left the last room to head up toward the radar housings, I took a moment to breathe in the fresh air and the scent of pine and fir and to admire the scenery I had grown up with but had, with age, taken for granted. At this point I caught a glimpse— only from the waist up and just for a second—of a young man with a crew cut in a white short-sleeved shirt; it was not a spooky ghostly image but appeared as solid as anyone who was there with me. This prompted me to turn on my voice recorder. Then, for the rest of my visit, I snapped pictures and asked a few questions of any spirits that may still have occupied the structure, being more interested in the visual appearance of the bunker than in any ghosts that might be present in or around it.

After leaving and returning home, I listened to my audio recordings and was astounded by what I had picked up: numerous EVPs, including a few instances of "Booyah!" and a young man saying, rather timidly, "They told me this . . . was home. . . ." But what impressed me and what still stands out as one of the most clear and almost chilling EVPs I have ever recorded was a man's deep voice saying "Respect in God," the reverberation bouncing off the cement walls. I listen to the EVP often, especially after visits to the bunker, and am always amazed by its clarity. I will always wonder if this is the voice of the young man I saw there that day.

I have been asked on numerous occasions for my thoughts and observations of the bunker, and my answer remains the same. I have had experiences and collected data on some visits and found nothing on other trips. The phenomena I have detected may very well just be fragments of history trapped within the sandstone surroundings, but they might also indicate the spirit of a dedicated soldier who remained behind to guard our coastline from

This World War II–era lookout bunker is nestled deep in the trees of a Cape Arago hiking trail.

enemy invasion. Whatever or whoever remains there is not a horror film, in-your-face-scary ghost, but rather someone who shows respect and deserves respect in return. But you can judge for yourself. And in an area filled with trails so rich in history, both military and American Indian, one would almost expect some other paranormal activity in the surrounding woods and many other nearby trails and hidden locations.

The trail is open to the public for day use and closes at dusk. It is a wonderful outing for the family, surrounded by nature and history. The bunker is a welcoming place to stop and rest, have lunch, and, before moving on up the trail, imagine what it was like in the 1940s. But before you leave, salute and thank the men who protected us. Some of them may very well still be able to hear you.

CHAPTER 19

Yaquina Bay Lighthouse
NEWPORT

YAQUINA BAY LIGHTHOUSE may often sit in the shadow of Heceta Head Lighthouse as far as legends and ghosts go, but it is not without its own unique structure and its fair share of paranormal activity.

The story of Yaquina Bay Lighthouse begins in 1869, when Henry W. Corbett asked that it be constructed at Newport, a populous port at the mouth of Yaquina Bay and along the busy West Coast shipping lanes between San Francisco and Puget Sound. Corbett presented to the Oregon state legislature his plan for a lighthouse to guide the heavy traffic going in and out of the bay, and the legislature approved it, purchasing 36 acres from local residents Lester and Sophrina Baldwin for $500 in gold in 1871 and officially beginning construction in May of that year.

Work went quickly, even by today's standards, under the guidance of Newport resident Ben Simpson. The guiding beacon, a whale-oil lamp within a fifth-order Fresnel lens, was lit for the first time on November 23, 1871. Yaquina Bay Lighthouse went from a vision to reality in just over six months.

The first and only lighthouse keeper at the site, Charles H. Peirce, a former US Army captain and veteran of the Civil War, arrived in Newport with his wife and six of his eight children. A ninth child was born in 1872 during their first year at Yaquina Bay Lighthouse.

Yaquina Bay Lighthouse remained active for a mere three years due to construction of the Heceta Head Lighthouse. Maritime traffic had increased considerably, and local officials decided that the area would be more safely served with the light at Yaquina Head, 4 miles to the north. So Yaquina Bay Lighthouse extinguished its beacon on October 1, 1874, and Charles Peirce and family moved along to Cape Blanco, where he would remain as lighthouse keeper for another 10 years.

As quickly as Yaquina Bay Lighthouse was built in the fall of 1871, it began to deteriorate, and in 1877 the Lighthouse Board wrote that the lighthouse was in "such wretched condition as to be almost uninhabitable." So the lighthouse remained unoccupied until 1888, when the US Army Corps of Engineers claimed it as home for John Polhemus, the engineer in charge of constructing the north and south jetties at Yaquina Bay. This project lasted until 1896, at which time the lighthouse once again became unoccupied.

One can assume that Polhemus was glad to move on. He and his family had experienced several brushes with death and injury during their stay at Yaquina Bay Lighthouse, with one severe enough to be reported in the *Morning Oregonian* newspaper on November 20, 1889.

"A thunder storm occurred here this morning, accompanied by some hail," the newspaper account read. "Lightning struck the old lighthouse building occupied by J. S. Polhemus, government engineer. The building was badly splintered and the furniture demolished. Mrs. Polhemus and child narrowly escaped."

Once more the lighthouse sat empty, until 1906, when the US Life-Saving Service used the building as quarters for its local crew. As with previous occupants, this group tried to restore what they could in the old lighthouse in order to make it feel more like home. A merger with the Revenue Cutter Service in 1915 formed the US Coast Guard, and that agency built an eight-story steel observation tower that remains at the site to this day. Then, in 1933, the USCG moved on, and the lighthouse was abandoned once again.

In 1934, a portion of the land, including the lighthouse, went to the state of Oregon on behalf of its highways and public parks. Yaquina Bay Lighthouse once again came to life with visitors and families enjoying the area for picnics, outings, and photographs of the newly completed Yaquina Bay Bridge.

As time passed and the lighthouse itself remained deserted, ghost stories became prevalent, but city officials would have none of it. In the 1930s and 1940s, ghosts were just not spoken of publicly, let alone a draw of any public place, so officials considered tearing down the old lighthouse and obliterating the ghost stories that went with it. Had it not been for the Lincoln County Historical Society that may well be what happened. For three years, the society tried to raise the funds needed to preserve the lighthouse but, sadly, failed to do so. Talks of tearing down the lighthouse turned into preparations, and its future looked bleak. Then along came a man named L. E. Warford. Taken by the lighthouse, he joined the preservation campaign and got national attention for the site. The fruits of Warford's determination were realized in 1955, when the plans to tear down the lighthouse were abandoned.

Finally finding its purpose, Yaquina Bay Lighthouse proudly served as a county museum for nearly two decades. It was also listed by the National Register of Historic Places in 1970. At this time, ownership was again transferred to the Oregon Parks and Recreation Department, and in 1974, the lighthouse was completely restored under the Historic Preservation Act. At last, on December 7, 1998, the lighthouse beacon was relit.

Yaquina Bay Lighthouse is the only existing wooden lighthouse in the state of Oregon, and it is the oldest structure in Newport, Oregon. It is also the only existing structure on the West Coast in which a lighthouse is built into the center of the light keeper's house, as opposed to others that have secondary and often distant living quarters.

As with any claims of an historical haunting—especially in a lighthouse—distinguishing fact from legend can be difficult. Documentation and records from the 1800s are few and far between, and personal experiences were typically taken to the grave. Nonetheless, the ghosts of Yaquina Bay Lighthouse seem plentiful and are still spoken of to this day.

According to the ghost stories associated with Yaquina Bay Lighthouse, it is haunted by a seaman named Evan MacClure, who was the captain of the whaling ship *Monkton*. In 1874, a powerful storm is reported to have struck the area and swept the hapless vessel into the Devil's Punchbowl, a large, natural bowl partially open to the Pacific Ocean that is carved into the rocky headland near the lighthouse. The ship wrecked. For more than a century, visitors, employees, and townsfolk have reported seeing an old captain standing at the base of the lighthouse and looking up, as though he were still trying to see the light that would guide him to safety. Those who have witnessed this say he appears as an older man and is as clear as any living person, until he suddenly vanishes before their eyes. Many residents say that MacClure continued to follow the light of the lighthouse and that his spirit occupied it, becoming a part of the beam and structure that led many a sailor to safe harbors.

Also in 1874, a ship sailed into the Newport harbor carrying a man who called himself Trevenard and who had brought his teenaged daughter Zina—or Muriel, depending on the teller of the tale—to visit with friends after her mother had passed away. Trevenard spent a few days in the little town with his daughter and then left her in a small hotel to continue her visit.

We can assume that in 1874 life was simpler and that teenagers were better behaved when left unattended than they are today. So it should not be too surprising that Zina/Muriel and her friends opted for a picnic lunch on the grass of Yaquina Bay Lighthouse. But teenagers being teenagers, they decided to investigate the interior of the lighthouse. According to the stories, they discovered a hidden room on the third floor and spent quite some time investigating it before leaving the lighthouse. When they once again reached the yard, Zina/Muriel realized she had left her handkerchief inside the building, so she left to retrieve it as her friends waited outside. After a few minutes, however, a scream pierced the air, and her friends hurried inside and followed a trail of blood drops that led them back to the third floor. As they looked for Zina/Muriel, they found only her bloodied handkerchief, and the unfortunate girl was never seen again—at least not alive. But there are those who claim her restless spirit still wanders the halls of Yaquina Bay Lighthouse, seeking a way out.

Even today, visitors to the lighthouse report eerie sensations and the feeling of being watched as they tour the building. Others have reported hearing whispering voices, both male and female, and seeing a flickering light on the second floor after dark. While most of the workers and volunteers in the lighthouse say they

Yaquina Bay Lighthouse is still a solitary and mysterious structure.

have not experienced any type of paranormal activity, there are those who have seen, heard, and felt an unseen presence.

My experiences at Yaquina Bay Lighthouse were not definitive, and I came away neither believing nor disbelieving the legends. But I will return there to attempt to shed some light on the truth of the ghost stories that have been passed down from generation to generation.

You may judge for yourself, however, any time you pass through Newport, Oregon, and decide to visit Yaquina Bay Lighthouse. Perhaps you will catch a glimpse of a young girl with a bloodstained handkerchief looking for a way out, or a sailor seeking the light. And even if you do not, you will be standing in a part of Oregon history.

Southern Oregon

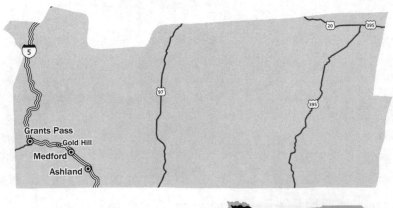

Ashland
  Lithia Park

Gold Hill
  Oregon Vortex

Grants Pass
  Schmidt House

Medford
  Darkwing Manor and
  Morguetorium

CHAPTER 20

Darkwing Manor and Morguetorium

MEDFORD

WHEN YOU ARE TRAVELING toward Medford, Oregon, you come to a fork in the road. Whichever way you take eventually leads you right into the bustling city of Medford, but if you go off the main and most traveled road, you take the scenic route. Instead of rest stops and speeding semis, you are treated to an unrepressed countryside dotted with turn-of-the-century homes, farms, and rusted vintage tractors used as decorations in fields. And one historic house always catches one's eye—Darkwing Manor and Morguetorium.

This stately and rather Gothic-looking house sits a bit back from the road, behind an elegant courtyard replete with towering poplar trees. During the Halloween season the house is often transformed into one of the most frightening haunts in Oregon, with all monies raised going to local charities. During the rest of the year, Darkwing Manor and Morguetorium is available for special events and paranormal investigation, and the extensive museum is open by appointment. Visitors know immediately when they step across the threshold that it will be an experience they will not soon forget.

George A. Hover, a devoted, God-fearing family man, had the Queen Anne–style house built in 1908 as a home for his wife and seven children. Even before the home was complete, Hover cultivated the land and planted fruit orchards. While his main crops were pears, peaches, and plums, he also successfully cultivated apples, cherries, and almonds, as well as vegetable crops such as potatoes and corn. He prepared his own fruit and vegetables for shipping to awaiting markets in the north and east of the United States. He was also the first to ship his peaches by express rail to Portland and eventually as far as New York, where his pears became award winning. The orchard was eventually named Valley View Orchards.

While Oregon has a reputation for rainy weather, it is also often a victim of drought, and after several crop failures at Valley View Orchards, Hover could no longer maintain his financial responsibilities to creditors. In 1917 the home was foreclosed on, and he lost it to John Hoppin of Minnesota. Then, in 1920, Hoppin deeded the Hover house and its property to Ira and Julia Canfield as a wedding gift. Ira Canfield was also a well-known orchardist, so the fruit trees persisted on some level.

The Canfields eventually had a daughter, Elizabeth, and their house became a home. But tragedy struck in 1931, when a young Elizabeth died from a ruptured appendix. This so devastated her parents that Elizabeth lay in state in the bay window of the living room for what was considered an excessive amount of time. Her bedroom and toy room were also sealed up and kept exactly the way Elizabeth had left them. They remained sealed for two decades and opened only to a few of Elizabeth's friends, who would occasionally come to the home and ask to see them. In such cases, the doors were cracked opened and the friends were allowed to peek in, but they were never allowed to enter.

The house changed hands a few more times over the decades, until it was purchased by current owners Tim and Tina Reuwsaat. They corrected many poor restoration attempts previous owners made, leaving as much original as possible. They also received visits from two of Elizabeth's childhood friends, who gifted them with some of the child's books, which they had received at her funeral.

The interior of Darkwing Manor is awe inspiring, filled with antiques, Gothic and exotic alike. Visitors will see hand-forged iron chandeliers featuring dragons and witches, portraits of Vlad the Impaler, gargoyles and bats, vintage toys, taxidermy animals, antique clothing, and everything in between. The Morguetorium, which is located in the room right off the living room, is interesting and creepy at the same time. All of its contents are authentic: 19th-century death photos, funeral attire and mourning jewelry, and even an antique infant casket. And, of course, there is the huge window in the living room in front of which Elizabeth lay in state after her death in 1951.

You will see more of the same outdoors, to include Gothic lighting fixtures and decor. And in the garage are two horse-drawn hearses, one dating to the era of the Civil War. (One of the most interesting pictures I have seen from Darkwing Manor, in fact, was one taken by Tina of one of the hearses, which clearly shows a ghostly veiled woman inside of it.) I can say in all honesty that concentrating on an investigation can be distracting when there is so much history and beauty to look at. But with a team as professional and focused as PSI of Oregon, I knew that the investigation would be top-notch even if I took an hour or two to absorb the beauty and history of the magnificent home.

I have been to Darkwing Manor with my team twice thus far for overnight investigations, and it has never disappointed. I recall, very vividly, our first visit—walking in to sit around the table in the kitchen, welcomed with coffee and Tina's amazing brownies, and hearing a little girl's voice say "Hello!" from the living room area. It was a disembodied voice as opposed to an EVP, and all but a few at the table stopped and turned toward where we had heard the voice. (A disembodied voice is an audible sound that you can hear at the time without the need for a digital voice recorder, while an EVP is electronic voice phenomena, voices or sounds you may not hear at the time but which you can hear when you play back a recording device). We all felt immediately that it was a curious Elizabeth wondering who we might be, and things only got better after that.

Because the house is in the countryside of Medford, it doesn't get much traffic or have close neighbors to interfere with audio or video recordings, so we investigated outside almost as much as we did inside. While we did not capture much on our cameras, we did hear a male disembodied voice as we were stepping onto the front porch that was so incredibly loud that it sent me running into the house ahead of everyone. It was a simple "Hey!" but the volume literally made my eardrums vibrate.

If I had to choose the most active place in Darkwing Manor, it would be the Morguetorium. It sits just off the living room and is everything its name suggests. To me, it is the perfect example of where tangible history and the paranormal come together. Beneath a glass-topped display case are various types of funeral announcements and a collection of antique mourning jewelry. Much of the jewelry contains hair of someone deceased for more than a century, many contain photos of the deceased, and some are beautifully hand-carved remembrances. Visitors will also see antique rosaries, small framed death photographs, bracelets, necklaces, and postcards.

While all this might seem morbid to some, I found it to be a fascinating learning experience about how the perception of death has changed over the decades. We carry these beautiful mementoes with us until we join our loved ones on the other side, and death seems to have gone from a personal transition to a commercial one. I found myself trying to imagine the woman holding the black lace handkerchief or wearing the pendant with her deceased husband's photograph and a lock of his hair in it. Far from being frightening to me it was quite beautiful.

My team and I spent a great deal of time in this room discussing whether or not one or more spirits could still be emotionally attached to these items, and our conclusion was that it was likely. Something that was carried for years with such emotion and love must have remnants of that energy. Shortly after that conversation, I snapped a photo of a teammate who was standing in the center of the room, and upon reviewing the photos, I saw my teammate with a glowing blue light that looked as though it began at her feet and was swirling up around her body. Perhaps that was our answer.

I have visited and investigated hundreds of locations in Oregon, and Darkwing Manor will always remain one of my favorite experiences. If I were asked to declare this house haunted or not, I would immediately and unequivocally say that it is. The ghosts that reside there are friendly and a few have great senses of humor. There is nothing dark or evil or oppressive in the house, and it is a history lesson awaiting your arrival.

Tim and Tina Reuwsaat are gracious, educated hosts who have always made us feel welcome in their home. Tina is an avid antique collector and, in my opinion, an expert on them. Aside from feelings and vivid dreams when she first moved in, Tina has not experienced paranormal activity and is very up front about that. She does not disbelieve; she just has not experienced what others have—although she is still baffled by the photo she took of the hearse that shows the spectral veiled woman inside. And my first impression of Tim was that he is the strong, silent type, with a great sense of humor; he is always helpful any way he can be and the most gracious host I have ever met.

Darkwing Manor and Morguetorium is a bundle of complementary experiences beneath one roof: history, antiques, the paranormal, and two of the greatest people you could ever hope to meet. So if you are passing through the Medford area, take the scenic route and see the manor firsthand. You will not be disappointed. And be sure to say hi to Elizabeth while you are there.

CHAPTER 21

Lithia Park
ASHLAND

IF YOU ARE TRAVELING to the Ashland area, you will not be at a loss for interesting and eclectic activities all year round. The Oregon Shakespeare Festival, which was just a summertime event for many years, now runs from February through October and includes plays by both its namesake and others in three different theaters. If shopping and sampling gourmet foods are your things, Ashland boasts hundreds of restaurants, art galleries, and specialty retail stores to catch your eye. And, of course, if it is ghosts you are seeking, you will have come to the right place, as nary a structure or outdoor location in Ashland does not have reports of hauntings. I have often wondered, in fact, if the ghosts outnumber the living.

Lithia Park is not only the largest and most centrally located park in Ashland, many say it is also one of the most haunted locations in the area. It is 93 acres of forested land around Ashland Creek, stretching from the downtown area up to the headwaters near Mount Ashland. It would take weeks for the average person to explore every nook and cranny of the park; many have tried, but few have succeeded.

Lithia Park was once the site of Abel Helman and Eber Emery's flour mill, the first building in what we now know as Ashland. The town grew up around the old facility, which was eventually abandoned by everyone but roaming livestock, became regarded as an eyesore, and was ultimately demolished to make way for Lithia Park.

The park has some pleasant distractions. Visitors will find a band shell for public concerts and plays, two duck ponds and a large playground for children, tennis courts and community buildings, miles and miles of hiking trails, and picnic areas. It even has an ice-skating rink in the wintertime. It truly is a family destination for many, and an historic destination for many more.

Lithia Park got its name from the chemical lithium oxide or lithia, an inorganic chemical compound that was discovered in the water pumped into the stream and in 1907 was deemed to not pose any health hazards. Journalist Bert Greer moved to Ashland in 1911 and purchased the *Ashland Tidings* newspaper. He wanted to establish a spa resort at Lithia Park, even campaigning for a bond issue in order to fund improvements related to mineral springs in the park, a measure that succeeded in 1914. During this time, controversy arose over how the funding was being spent and who had control over the park. As a result of this, control of Lithia Park was returned to the parks commission in 1916. The commission dropped the mineral springs resort idea and turned its attention to improving the park's landscaping features and introducing many native and nonnative plants.

Lithia Park fell into a state of disrepair after 1937, lack of funding caused many parts of it to succumb to decay, and vandalism destroyed many landmarks.

In 1974, the park was hit by a devastating flood that wrecked much of its landscaping, and several years passed before repairs were completed and improvements to the drainage system were made. These upgrades were nonetheless not enough to ward off another flood in 1997, which caused even more destruction to the park and to the nearby historic shopping and dining area known as Ashland Plaza. Repairs and additional work around Lithia Creek over the following years have hopefully increased protection from future flooding. Today Lithia Park is the natural centerpiece for the city of Ashland. On warm summer nights it hosts concerts, plays, and many other free public events, and during the day it provides hours of entertainment for children in the large playground and plenty of shaded picnic areas for the entire family.

Any location so replete with history, good and bad, is likely haunted, and Lithia Park has ghosts aplenty. Documentation from the earliest days of Ashland is nearly nonexistent, so research to support this claim is fruitless. Some say the stories of ghosts are just legends, but when you find so many credible firsthand accounts, you tend to believe the legends might be based on actual phenomena.

Many a visitor has encountered the ghost of a young girl who is said to have been raped and murdered in 1875 at the site where Lithia Park now sits, and according to reports from over the past century, she most often manifests as a radiating blue light or a misty form in a dress.

One of the most retold accounts of the blue light is from 1975, when a vacationing family suddenly saw it while driving along one of the winding roads in the park and, unable to stop,

*It is under the small, dim, summer star. / I know not who these mute folk are /
Who share the unlit place with me— / Those stones out under the low-limbed
tree / Doubtless bear names that the mosses mar.*
—Robert Frost, "Ghost House"

passed right through it. Shaken, they pulled over, unsure of what
they had seen and passed through and seeing nothing behind
them. All recalled feeling a sharp, damp coldness as they passed
through the blue light, however, and this is a common sensation
when one encounters a ghost.

The blue light or blue mist-like apparition of the girl has
been reported hundreds of times and has also been seen hovering over the duck ponds; many eyewitnesses have compared it
to a flickering flame or described it as pulsating, and they generally say it is visible for between 30 seconds and 2 minutes.

Then, just as quickly as it appears, the light is suddenly snuffed out. I believe this could be an indication of what the young girl experienced in death, that she had a vibrant energy in life that was doused in a violent way and that perhaps this is her way of communicating that to those who see her.

Another commonly recounted experience is that of a dog-faced boy, so called because he suffered from the disease called hypertrichosis, informally called werewolf syndrome. This is a real malady that has afflicted thousands of people worldwide and that causes abnormal amounts of hair to grow over the entire body, including the face. In the 1920s, however, in the absence of medical explanations, one can imagine how terribly a young boy may have been treated.

Various accounts through the decades suggest that the boy lived on his own from a very early age because he was an embarrassment to his parents. With no means of support, financially or emotionally, he resorted to selling pencils on street corners and stealing from unlocked cars or yards. He was always seen with a gunnysack flung over his shoulder to carry his wares and illegal acquisitions. Then, in 1926, the boy suddenly vanished, and many speculate that he was murdered. Extralegal punishments such as hangings were commonplace in Oregon during this time, so even though his body was never found, this is certainly a possible explanation.

In the 1960s, there were a rash of reports of a dog-faced boy with a gunnysack in Lithia Park near where the young boy had once been active and, strangely, items once again started to disappear from unlocked cars. Local police were summoned to the area many times, but by the time they arrived the boy was nowhere to be found and baffled witnesses said it seemed as though he could appear and disappear at will. To this day, many people swear it is the ghost of the dog-faced boy that disappeared under mysterious circumstances nine decades ago.

Yet another ghost that many still whisper about today is that of a logger who was crushed to death when a tree fell in the wrong direction in the 1940s. He was reportedly well known in the community for his logging skills, as well as for using his drinking jug as a makeshift musical instrument. It is said that he could blow out any song he chose on his jug, which—if you have ever tried to use an empty bottle to play a song—is no easy feat. He has been described as a big, burly man, but sweet as a teddy bear and helpful to friends and strangers alike. Throughout the years there have been numerous reports from other loggers in the area who say they have been pushed or pulled from the path of a falling tree that they never saw coming. In most of the reports, the loggers who were saved from a horrible death claim to have heard the sounds of someone blowing out a song on a jug just prior to the incident. In the dangerous job of logging, having a musically inclined guardian logger is something that is not feared but, rather, welcomed.

I have been to Lithia Park many times and have found it soothing and humbling to be surrounded by the flowing water and by trees that have lived there for hundreds of years. It makes me smile to see children laughing and playing and couples hiking hand in hand. Because I like to consider myself an artist and photographer, my favorite time to visit Ashland and Lithia Park is in the autumn, when colors come alive and there is an icy nip to the air. I have never stayed after dark, so I have not had the chance to witness the floating blue light, nor have I seen the dog-faced boy or the logger. But I have heard what sounded like someone blowing out a tune on a jug. Could this have been just the winds catching a bottle that had been discarded somewhere? Certainly. But, on the flip side, it also could have been the kindly guardian logger making his presence known. Either way, I said hello. I hope you will, too, when you visit the park.

CHAPTER 22

Oregon Vortex
GOLD HILL

FOR THOSE SEEKING A GOOD HAUNTING, the Oregon Vortex fits that bill. But there is a bit more to the Oregon Vortex than ghosts, a more visual type of unexplained activity involving gravity, magnetism, and fluctuations in size that has left thousands of visitors speechless and at a loss for a natural explanation.

The Oregon Vortex is everything that legends are made of—especially local legends. And according to locals, a building constructed by the Old Grey Eagle Mining Company in 1904 was dislodged from its foundation by heavy rain and subsequent mudslides and came to rest at the odd angle that it still sits at today. During its heyday as a gold assay office, miners would frequent the building to have their gold weighed and were baffled many times by scale readings that, more often than not, seemed wildly off. This was commonplace until 1910, when the mudslide put the office out of business.

American Indians living nearby were wary of the site, calling it the "Forbidden Ground." They claimed their horses would stop suddenly and refuse to enter the site, and as a result, they did too. Local wildlife is rarely found within the area, and trees grow at an incline toward magnetic north.

In the late 1920s, a geologist named John Litster moved to the area and was so taken aback by what he saw that he remained there for the rest of his life, performing tests, developing theories, and attempting to solve the strange riddle. Litster believed that the area contained a strange energy field that somehow warped the boundaries of space and time. In 1930 he opened the ground as a public attraction while he continued to delve into the mysteries, right up to the time of his death in 1959.

Today there are believers and skeptics when the subject turns to the Oregon Vortex. Some of the former will tell you that there is a spherical area of force that measures nearly 165 feet in diameter and sits halfway above the ground and halfway below the ground. This force, or vortex, lays directly within the property lines. Depending on where they stand, those inside the vortex appear to shrink or grow larger. It also causes balls to roll uphill with no physical assistance and compasses to spin wildly. Even brooms stand upright. Another claim is that those standing inside the vortex will feel as though they are standing upright, but they are actually leaning at an angle of 7.5 degrees. Because of this, many have reported a feeling of vertigo or dizziness while enveloped in the sphere. Inevitably, visitors seem to lean at an angle toward magnetic north.

It had been nearly two decades since I had visited the Oregon Vortex, so my memories of any experiences there were quite faded and I deliberately avoided doing any research into claims before embarking on the two-hour drive from the coast to Gold Hill. While I believe in and have experienced the paranormal and unexplained, I always try to maintain an attitude of skepticism while investigating any location.

As a tour guide led us through the property, I listened and took notes, watched the demonstrations, and observed the apparent height changes and seeming lack of gravity that causes objects to roll uphill and which the vortex is most famous for.

Strangely, the height differences are seen largely in photographs and not so much with the naked eye. There are literally hundreds of photographs, past and present, all over the Internet of the astounding change in height between two people. Could it all have been an optical illusion? Quite possibly, since the building and everything around it is on a slant. Could it be that there is something in the magnetic field that alters one's height and makes objects travel uphill? Again, it is possible. Just because we cannot see it does not mean it does not exist. I will admit to queasiness as I neared the 165-foot-circle and experiencing a dull, throbbing, dizzying headache. While this is not unusual for me, it was unusual that it ceased the farther away from the circle I walked.

The Oregon Vortex is more, however, than height changes and dizziness, and many believe the house itself to be haunted by the ghost of John Litster. He did, after all, live and die on the property, and he devoted his life to experiments and theories on the strange occurrences, angles, and experiments. It was his home and, by all accounts, he loved it. A few people I spoke with who made regular visits to the vortex reported having seen an apparition in the old tilted house. Some saw a man and some saw a brief shadow. Many have seen him leaning casually against a wall, watching tourists express amazement over his home, and others see a fleeting shadow or white mist along the wooded grounds.

Naturally, I turned on my voice recorder during the time I spent in the house (although I found out later this was not allowed because of copyright issues), but the voices of many excited visitors washed away anything I may have recorded. Personally, I did not see or hear anything paranormal, but as every paranormal researcher knows, it is rare to do so. Many people I have spoken with are adamant about what they have experienced at the Oregon Vortex, and who am I to doubt them without proof?

So if you find yourself in Oregon, looking for an awe-inspiring way to spend a day, consider taking a drive to Gold Hill and follow the signs to the Oregon Vortex. Then grow a few inches, shrink a few inches, and maybe see the ghost of John Litster.

CHAPTER 23

Schmidt House

GRANTS PASS

THE OREGON TRAIL is a 2,000-mile, historic east-west wagon route used by early settlers of the West that was blazed by fur trappers and traders between about 1811 and 1840. Originally it was only passable by foot or horseback, but as the years passed, the trail was made more easily accessible to wagon trains. Ultimately, almost 400,000 settlers, ranchers, farmers, businessmen, and miners moved themselves and their families on the Oregon Trail to the areas that were to become Oregon and California.

Death on the Oregon Trail was common. An estimated 10,000 to 20,000 travelers died on the trek, from causes ranging from disease to accidents, hypothermia, and American Indian attacks. The exact number of those lost on the Oregon Trail is not known because the dead were often buried in unmarked graves right on the roadway—and as draft animals continued to trample the trail and pack the earth more firmly, the graves became impossible to detect.

It was because of these dangers that Jesse Applegate led a small group of trailblazers in search of a safer southern route of passage. This route later became known as the Applegate Trail or South Emigrant Road, and along it Claus and Hannachen Schmidt traveled to the Rogue Valley.

A farmer originally hailing from Denmark, Claus Schmidt arrived with his wife Hannachen and began farming in Grants Pass in 1887. After only a few years, however, the Alaskan Gold Rush became so appealing that he left Grants Pass alone and headed for Alaska. Once there, he worked as a cook for the miners until he had saved enough money to return home to Grants Pass and open a small store.

Claus and Hannachen remained for some time on the farm they had purchased years earlier, but in 1901 Claus had a small four-room house constructed in town, crafted from locally made bricks and conveniently located within walking distance of his store. As the Schmidt family grew, they constructed a wood-shingled addition, transforming the small house into a stately two-story home by 1910.

Both Claus and Hannachen passed away in the late 1920s, but their daughters continued living in the home, with Anna Schmidt and her brother Herman running the family store until 1949 and Flora working for a local bank.

In 1978, the Schmidt sisters gifted the home to the Josephine County Historical Society, and in 1983, it was opened as a museum. The beautiful house is still very much the Schmidt home, containing the original furniture, toys, and even some goods from the family store, allowing visitors to take a step back in time when they step through the doorway.

The Schmidt family resided in the home from the time of its construction in 1901 until it was donated to the Josephine County Historical Society. During those 77 years, at least three members of the Schmidt family died in the home. Hannachen died in 1925, Claus passed away in 1927, and their son Herman died in 1949. Anna and Flora never married and remained together in the home, sharing the same bedroom overlooking 5th Street for most of the 20th century. In the early 1980s, the sisters moved into a nursing home, where they remained until their deaths, Flora in 1981 at 87 years old, and Anna in 1987 at 99 years old.

Some remain skeptical that the Schmidt house is haunted, while others gladly recount stories of strange sounds, whispers, and fast-moving shadows seen out of the corners of their eyes. The most commonly reported sightings are those of a shadowy figure near upstairs bedroom doorways and a "wispy, white, smoke-like" figure at various points throughout the house.

In 2009, my paranormal research team, PSI of Oregon, was invited to investigate the Schmidt House. Prior to setting up equipment, we toured the house and took in the amazing memories of the Schmidt family. Family photographs were displayed everywhere, as well as mementos such as high school diplomas and vintage knickknacks. Upstairs is a room that contains the Schmidt children's many toys—dolls and dollhouses, train sets, teddy bears, and many books. A sewing room houses needle-work, quilts, and clothing made by the Schmidt women, as well as the original treadle-foot sewing machine. The bedroom of Claus and Hannachen Schmidt is adorned with photographs, clothing worn by Hannachen, and the bed the couple shared. Anna and Flora's room is at the end of the hallway with two beds and a lovely vanity, vintage hats and hatboxes, and the sisters' clothing. Downstairs, nestled in the kitchen, is the family's original wood-burning cooking stove, and the living room is home to an old piano and also serves as an exhibition room in which the historical society periodically changes out the displays.

After the tour we began to set up our equipment and settled in for the night—and an interesting night it would be.

Most of the sounds throughout the house were tracked and attributed to settling or gusts of wind; even the sound of distant traffic carried and echoed within the walls. But there were other distinct sounds that we could not attribute to a mundane source. Some were audible words and groans that were heard by more than one member of our team and captured on our digital voice recorders, while others were caught only on the recorders and revealed on playback. A male voice was recorded clearly asking "Who are you?" and two different female voices were recorded saying "Hello" and "I see you." Downstairs near the piano a young male voice was recorded laughing.

In Anna and Flora's room, we placed a K-II meter, a type of electromagnetic field (EMF) meter, on one of the beds and asked a series of yes-or-no questions. As the lights of the K-II meter began to seemingly respond to the questions, we took a series of photographs of the meter on the bed in rapid succession. When we reviewed these photographs after the investigation, we saw a dark, circular shadow clearly passing over the meter. We wondered, and still wonder today, if the correlation of the responses on the K-II meter, the EVP we recorded, and the shadow might have indicated the presence of one of the Schmidt sisters.

We photographed some other interesting images that night in Grants Pass, including a wispy white figure and another shadow in the living room. My team has not been able to explain these images, but because there may be a natural explanation, we have not judged them to be definitively paranormal. While we believe in ghosts and hauntings, we remain skeptical enough to know that all that looks paranormal is not necessarily so. As far as the

Schmidt House is concerned, however, we agreed that someone or more than one person not of this realm still resides there.

"It was an amazing investigation and an amazing opportunity to glimpse life in the early 20th century," said PSI of Oregon cofounder Laura Schier. "We certainly cannot explain everything we saw and heard. But I can say that the Schmidt House is still one of our favorite investigations of all time."

The Schmidt House was placed on the National Register of Historic Places on January 21, 2004. Whether you are interested in a grand piece of Oregon history, possibly catching a glimpse of a welcoming ghost, or both, the Schmidt House Museum is definitely worth visiting.

Central Oregon

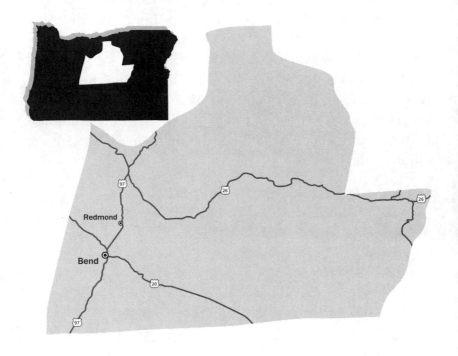

Bend
  McCann House
  O'Kane Building
  Old St. Francis School

Redmond
  Redmond Hotel

CHAPTER 24

McCann House
BEND

IN PUBLICATIONS from the West Coast to the East Coast, the site known variously as the McCann House and the Congress House—the latter because it sits on Congress Street—is listed among the five most haunted houses in the United States. Interestingly enough, while the lore associated with its hauntings seems to be known worldwide, the history of the house itself is limited. This prompted me to research the nomination forms submitted to the National Register of Historic Places— on which the house was listed in 1980—and to discover some wonderful information on the house, its tenants, and the ghosts that might be found within it.

Built between 1915 and 1916, the McCann House is a fine example of Georgian Revival architecture in what was at that time the small and isolated pioneer town of Bend. Shelvin-Hixon Lumber Company, which owned the lumber mill that provided the basis of Bend's economy, built the home for Thomas McCann, a longstanding employee of the family-oriented business who had become its vice president and general manager.

McCann and his family were the first to occupy the house upon its completion in 1916, and they remained there until 1921. They were the proud parents of young children, and there was a nursery that adjoined the master bedroom and allowed them to remain close to their children at all times. Features of the house also included servants' quarters on the third floor, a bell summoning system, and a modern central vacuum system in the basement, with outlets on the first and second floors. Another unique feature of the house was a wooden box with a false bottom that was operated with hand pulleys to bring firewood upstairs. And these are just a few of the many noteworthy features of the house that are still intact and operational today.

McCann was attentive to the needs of his employees. He established a company newspaper called the *Shelvin Equalizer* and provided his workers with schools for their children, a hospital, and a high standard of housing.

When McCann was elected vice president of Shelvin-Hixon's parent company in St. Paul, Minnesota, the house was taken over by J. P. Hennessy, who lived there with his family for four years. Hennessy had arrived in Bend at the same time as McCann and assumed the position of sales manager and assistant general manager.

Following Hennessy in 1925 was C. L. Isted, who came aboard as general manager of Crookston Lumber Company, a partner of Shelvin-Hixon. Isted personally helped many families during the Great Depression and was instrumental in keeping the plant operating by avoiding a strike. He retired in 1944.

The final general manager of the Shelvin-Hixon plant was Hardy Meyers, who came to Bend with his family from Mississippi in 1944. Meyers was involved in numerous local civic organizations and was also a member of the board of directors for St. Joseph's Hospital. He was also the director of a local savings and loan company.

Somewhere along the line, people started to talk about a curse that had been placed on the home and land, and it has been blamed for the many people who have perished during their tenancy in the home. I have not been able to find anything unnatural about the deaths in the home—but the land and Bend itself are another story.

Sometimes bad things happen in small towns, and they travel through history with a bit of embellishment. But even if one stays true to the official account, it seems that Bend, and the areas around the McCann House, have seen more than their fair share of gruesome tragedy. Two unsolved murders in nearby Drake Park have been investigated and reinvestigated over the decades with no results, and many believe these murders have contributed to the hauntings at the McCann House.

On February 1, 1962, 17-year-old Judy Reeder was an attractive and popular homecoming queen and high school senior at Bend High School. As she often did, Judy drove her 1955 Ford sedan downtown and parked it on Riverside Boulevard. She was never seen alive again, and her body was found in Drake Park. The next day, as children arrived to play, two children discovered Judy's body beneath a footbridge, partially submerged in 4 inches of water. She had been struck in the head at least 13 times with a blunt object. Authorities at the time concluded that Judy had been dragged to a spot close to the rock retaining wall of the park's

Mirror Pond, but there the trail ended; they had no explanation how she got into the water, and the murder weapon was never found. To date, more than 500 witnesses and former boyfriends have been interviewed by police, but they are no closer to solving the crime than they were more than 50 years ago.

On April 30, 1979, a public works employee found a human thigh on the grates at the north end of Drake Park. A diving team subsequently searched Mirror Pond and recovered some additional body parts, but 47-year-old Mary Jo Templeton, a waitress and regular patron of local bars, was not completely reassembled until months later, when the last of her was pulled from the water. In 1988, police discovered that the manner in which Mary Jo was murdered was similar to four homicides in Tennessee, none of which have ever been solved.

But probably the most talked-about and gruesome murders were those of three Bend trappers at Little Lava Lake in 1924, still Deschutes County's largest multiple murder and its oldest cold case.

Three men—50-year-old Ed Nichols, 35-year-old Roy Wilson, and 24-year-old Dewey Morris—had decided to spend the winter trapping as a team, making their headquarters in a small log cabin at Little Lava Lake. The men seemed to be doing well with their chilly work, and around Christmas, a jovial Nichols pulled into Bend, announced that trapping had been good that year, and sold a sled load of valuable furs. By the time April rolled around, however, there had been no further word from the trappers. Suspicions were aroused immediately when searchers entered the isolated little cabin the three men had shared and found pots on the stove filled with burnt food and dishes on the table set for the untouched meal. The heavy sled used by the trappers was also missing.

As they continued to investigate the property, the searchers came upon a bloody hammer in the corner of an animal pen behind the house. They then began a search for the trap lines and discovered the frozen remains of twelve marten, four foxes, and a skunk in unattended traps. This is not something one would ever expect to find from experienced trappers whose livelihood depended upon retrieving pelts. The sheriff and game warden were called in to head up the search.

The next day the trapper's sled was discovered partially buried in a snowdrift. Human blood was found on the sled boards. Discouraged at not finding the trappers, the searchers had begun the trek back to the cabin when they stumbled across a patch of blood buried beneath the snow but still visible to the naked eye. As they began frantically digging into the snow, they found more blood, a tooth, and human hair. The ice on the lake was starting to melt and, when they discovered the rowboat in the snow that night, they launched it, eventually finding three decomposing bodies on the still-frozen surface.

"Hastily tying ropes to the corpses, the grim procession headed for shore," Sheriff Claude McCauley wrote about the grim discovery. "Here the bodies were fastened to the shelf ice for the night. Adams donned his snowshoes and made for town on the run."

The murders made headlines throughout Oregon, particularly in Bend.

"Even though the weather was perfect, the clear air was impregnated with the odor of death and decomposition and it was with an undefinable spirit of awe and consternation that the little party of hardy outdoorsmen laid aside their packs, kicked off their snowshoes, and prepared to tackle a grim job which was little to their liking," the sheriff continued.

Examination revealed that three separate instruments had been used on each of the victims—a shotgun, a pistol, and a blunt object that was most likely a hammer—but there were no immediate leads on who had killed the men.

In 1933, a man by the name of Lee Collins, who was also known by the more common alias of Charles Kimzey, was arrested for the murders. Although he maintained his innocence, he had had a falling out with one of the trappers and had been seen carrying a pack of pelts to a fur company in Bend shortly after Christmas of 1924. Collins pleaded not guilty to the murder charges but was found guilty on all counts by a jury of his peers and sentenced to life imprisonment in the Oregon State Penitentiary.

Many say the ghosts of the murder victims haunt both the land on which the McCann House sits and Bend overall. Gruesome, instant deaths are often the cause for hauntings, and some speculate that often the victims of these crimes have perished so quickly that they do not realize they are dead.

The McCann House itself seems to also have visible and audible ghosts. Many who have walked past the old home on one of the many walking tours that include it have seen shadowy male and female figures standing in an upstairs room from the street below. And many say that the ghosts of people who have died in the house wander not only the halls indoors but also the grounds outside.

"I don't know what I saw," one young man I spoke with said. "I mean, it was dark and shaped like a little kid and running across the lawn, but there was no substance to it, if that makes sense. And I have heard crying, very sad crying. And this is just the outdoor group tours. I have come by on my own a few times and have heard the same crying. It's a girl. And there always seem to be shadows somewhere. I can't say they are all ghosts, no, but they were very real to me."

People speak of the curse, but no one seems to have any definite information on it or what it was or why the house might have been cursed in the first place.

"Curses-schmurses," one older Bend resident told me. "Bad luck is bad luck, and we all die sometime. Might as well die at home where we like being!"

I have not personally seen or heard anything at the old McCann House, but that certainly does not mean that the ghosts others have seen and heard do not exist, just that my timing was not right. Most of the Bend residents I have spoken with, in fact, have either seen or heard evidence of the hauntings at the McCann House, or heard stories about them, and many of them believe these accounts. With such a sordid history of death and murder in Bend, I find the hauntings not just plausible but likely; the history itself makes it almost impossible for there not to be a bit of it left behind to speak to us. And if you partake in one of the town historical or haunted walking tours while in Bend, be sure to speak back to the McCann House.

CHAPTER 25

O'Kane Building

BEND

THE HEADLINES in the November 22, 1916, edition of the *Bend Bulletin* announced "Central Oregon's Finest Business Block. New O'Kane Building is modern type. Cost is estimated at $50,000. Offices are large and well-lighted. Mr. O'Kane's apartments neat." Yes, it was that remarkable!

The two-story O'Kane Building is an historic commercial building in Bend, and it is said that more than 300,000 bricks were needed to complete its construction. It originally housed the short-lived Dream Theater, a drugstore, and 20 apartments and office spaces. After the Dream Theater closed, the Palace Saloon took over its space and was successful for many years. No photos exist of the original theater, so when that part of the building was remodeled in 1985, it was done to match the rest of the structure.

Located on the corner of Oregon Avenue and Bond Street and facing both of them, the O'Kane Building has been in continuous use since it opened its doors a century ago. The 26,000-square-foot building was designed by the Breeze Brothers of Seattle, Washington, constructed with reinforced concrete, and considered very modern for its time. It was listed in the National Register of Historic Places in 1986 and is still the largest commercial building in Bend.

The month after the building was completed, Deschutes County broke away from Crook County, and Bend became the county seat of the new jurisdiction, which, initially, had no courthouse. So the new government leased two offices in the O'Kane Building, and they served as the first county courthouse for a year until a proper facility was constructed by the Deschutes County Investment Company.

Constructed in a mercantile style, the O'Kane Building has a flat roof with large display windows on the first floor, above which are stained-glass transom windows and decorative green tile borders, and good-sized office windows on the second floor. The main entrance to the building is considered its most beautiful architectural feature, with hand-carved wooden doorframes and, set in a circular frame in the center of the stained glass above it, the yellow-and-black Bend Bee. Bend is known for its many beekeepers, and images of bees appear all over town. The

Bend Bee is the same one depicted on the jars of honey produced by the Bend Bee Company.

In 1857, when he was just 12 years old, Hugh O'Kane stowed away on a ship bound for New York City, leaving behind his native Ireland and family there. He was an adventurous child with big dreams and high hopes. In no time he had set up shop and was shining the shoes of businessmen on the sidewalks of New York City. Over the following years he worked as a tailor, boxer, wrestler, miner, stagecoach driver, and mule packer, among other things, becoming the archetype of the jack-of-all-trades, and also engaged in some shadier pursuits, such as gambling and smuggling alcohol. In the 1870s, he packed up and moved to North Dakota, where he packed supplies for the US Army during its campaign against the Sioux Indians. Later he mined for gold, earning a sizable $50,000 fortune that he immediately gambled away.

O'Kane made yet another career change in 1881, when he became the manager for a world championship Greco-Roman wrestler named Tom Cannon. This seemed to interest him longer than most of his previous jobs, and he led Cannon's wrestling troupe on a 14-month tour of Europe and many exhibition shows. Sports were in his blood, and he later managed Ed Skinner and Marley Kettleman as they toured Australia as champion sprinters. Hugh O'Kane had one adventure after another, and nothing he did or attempted to do came as a shock to anyone.

In 1895, O'Kane married Helen Wright, and they settled down in Idaho—briefly. But that same year he opened a large hotel in Grangeville, Idaho, and no sooner had the ink dried on the purchase contract than O'Kane was off and running again, leaving his new wife to manage the establishment while he traveled around the country as a jockey, racing horses. Both the hotel and the horse racing turned into successful businesses for the O'Kanes.

O'Kane's restless spirit began to get the best of him, and in 1903, he packed up his belongings and, with his wife by his side for once, traveled to Oregon and settled in Bend. That same year O'Kane built the Bend Hotel, and it was an immediate success with local businessmen, civic leaders, and weary travelers and quickly became a central Oregon landmark. But on August 30, 1915, a fire broke out and destroyed the lavish hotel. O'Kane, however, was undeterred and unstoppable. What some may have accepted as a devastating loss, O'Kane saw as a wonderful opportunity to develop a vacant lot in a prime location. He hired the Breeze Brothers to design a fireproof building that could accommodate retail stores, offices, and apartments and completed his new venture, the O'Kane Building, in 1916.

O'Kane was a colorful man who had a great sense of humor and loved telling stories of his adventures to anyone who would listen to them. By the time he moved into the building bearing his name, O'Kane had ballooned to more than 300 pounds and was in declining health, having spent many a hot and humid afternoon outside his building in his lounge chair, puffing on his cigars and chatting with passersby. He passed away in Portland on February 16, 1930, after being noticeably ill for a mere 14 hours. The great adventurer had moved on to the greatest adventure of all, and his wife followed him five years later.

People in Bend still know O'Kane, and his name brings smiles to the faces even of those far too young to have known him. By all accounts he was a jolly man with a heart of gold. He left a legacy of buildings, was supportive both spiritually and financially of the Catholic Church, and even stood up against the Ku Klux Klan. People knew his stories were exaggerated, but many say that is why he was so loved and he never stopped entertaining.

Today, the O'Kane Building is in use at the heart of downtown Bend just as it was in 1916. Retail displays grace the big windows, office phones ring upstairs, and the smell of home cooking flows out the open windows of the apartment, all of which would surely make Hugh O'Kane smile proudly. There are 19 offices along the second floor corridor and, at the far end of the hall and overlooking Bond Street, is the apartment suite where Mr. and Mrs. O'Kane lived. Many believe that O'Kane loved the building so much, in fact, that he never left. It was his pride and joy, after all, so what better place for him to spend eternity?

Business owners, customers, and tenants have all long reported seeing puffs of smoke that seem to come from nowhere and smelling the strong odor of cigar smoke in various spots in the building.

"We've never had a fire here as far as I know, and I never hear the smoke alarms go off," one employee of a retail shop told me. "But every now and then I'll see a big old puff of smoke come from around a corner and think I need to go tell someone there is no smoking in here. But when I go look, there is nobody there, just the smoke and the smell of cigars. After a few times you get used to it, and I personally think it's old man O'Kane having fun with us. I don't mind. It's kind of cool that he might still be here. Most everyone around here has seen that or seen something else, but no one really gets scared or anything. We all have a pretty good idea who it is."

Along with the ghostly puffs of smoke, people have reported voices when no one else is in a room, disembodied footsteps, and strange glowing orb-like lights that seem to hang in the air before disappearing. In the ground-floor restaurant, after customers have left for the night, staff has reported hearing a woman's voice calling out orders. Perhaps someone else who spent time at the O'Kane Building loved it as much as Hugh O'Kane did and also chose to stick around in the afterlife. And in the basement, many have reported seeing an apparition of a short, heavyset man.

"I've seen him a few times," another employee told me. "It's always so quick and you can never really see his face, but you can

This marker is set into the wall of the historic O'Kane Building.

make out the body size. We've all seen the old man's pictures, and I would bet my last dollar that's who it is. A lot of people would scream and run, but I find excuses to go down there and maybe get the chance of seeing him again and making out his face. . . . Scary? No, not at all. Everyone who has seen him down there or somewhere else in the building always just smiles and says, 'Hi, Hugh!'"

I, too, would bet my last dollar that O'Kane is still keeping an eye on his building and trying to tell his stories to anyone willing to listen. Indeed, I would have to say that Bend overall is potentially one of the most haunted towns I have ever visited. And with an active ghost like Hugh O'Kane, it is not lacking for humor either.

CHAPTER 26

Old St. Francis School

BEND

OLD ST. FRANCIS SCHOOL was the first Irish-Catholic
school in central Oregon, opening in 1936, and the *Bend Bulletin* published a preliminary announcement regarding it several
years earlier, on May 29, 1925:

*Grade Building to Cost $45,000 Will Be Erected At Once on
Site of Present Parish House*

*Held in abeyance pending the decision of the Supreme Court on
the constitutionality of the Oregon school law, plans for the immediate construction in Bend of a parochial school costing approximately
$45,000, with equipment, was announced this morning by Father
Luke Sheehan, pastor of St. Francis Catholic Church.*

It was quite the trek from County Cork, Ireland, to Bend,
Oregon, for Father Luke Sheehan. He arrived in Bend in 1910
with the Irish Capuchin Order of Catholic Priests as part of a
mission into the wilds of Oregon, and once there, he rooted and
refined St. Francis Parish. He traveled hundreds of miles repeatedly, often on foot, to meet with parishioners scattered across the
state, many of whom were Irish countrymen who had also made
the trek to Oregon. He traveled bumpy roads in the winter to
bring Christmas meals and prayer to those who could not make
it into town to feast and worship. As much as he was a man of
the cloth, he was also an outdoorsman, a friend to all he met,
and a counselor and mentor to many. His hand was extended to
all, be they near to him or far across rugged terrain.

Father Sheehan, along with his nephew Father Dominic
O'Connor, prepared the ground and laid a solid foundation for
their dream, the St. Francis School. They did this during the
Great Depression, and many still say they had the power of God
on their side as they forged ahead with their plans for the school.
Their hard work manifested in a common-looking brick school-
house with four classrooms. Within a year of its opening, St.
Francis held nearly 150 students, from grades one to eight. As
the years went on, the number of active students increased to
more than 300, and St. Francis had a waiting list for enrollments.

To accommodate the students and the awaiting students,
two additional classrooms were added to the school in 1953, and

as the number of students continued to increase, another four classrooms were built in 1960. In 1968 even larger additions were added for much-needed space, including a new parish center to house a gymnasium, a stage, meeting rooms, and a cafeteria—the school became a centerpiece for the city of Bend.

The nuns who taught at St. Francis School came to Bend primarily from Marylhurst University, nine miles south of Portland, and were all part of the order known as the Sisters of the Holy Names of Jesus and Mary. Many of us have heard horror stories of overly strict nuns in school environments, but this was not the case at St. Francis School. Yes, the nuns expected a student's best efforts, but they are said to have had big hearts and to have truly cared for each and every one of their students.

By the time the late 1960s rolled around, the school was taking a more relaxed approach to education. School uniforms were no longer required, and even the nuns gave up their habits for more casual, secular clothing. Despite the relaxation in discipline, however, the school remained focused on education.

In 2000, the school was relocated to a more modern campus site, and the original school was renovated and repurposed into a hotel, several pubs, a theater, and even a smoking room, while the old five-bedroom parish house, four-bedroom nunnery, two-bedroom art house, and three-bedroom friary were converted into cabins that are available for rent. What visitors experience now is a wonderful combination of the creative and the unconventional. A walking tour of the property gives visitors a glimpse of the past, and how the grounds evolved into the present. Historical photos that pay homage to the Catholic beginnings of the school and original art based on stories about it are displayed throughout. Those who are sensitive to paranormal phenomena cannot help but feel their presence and sense that the place has stories to tell those to who are not afraid to hear them.

The entryway to the revived Old St. Francis School leads into the pub. Some of the first things visitors see when they enter are carved wooden relief panels inlaid with brass and huge skylights that seem like passageways to the stars. Other details visitors may note include small orange and cream drinking lights, a big 10-light candelabra chandelier, a cast-iron wood-burning stove to keep the room warm on cold winter evenings, backlit stained glass, etched windows, and a portrait of Father Luke Sheehan.

Other amenities visitors will find at Old St. Francis School include a smoking room, the Firelight Bar, a former meeting place for the Knights of Columbus, and even a Turkish bath. There is also O'Kanes, which offers local beer and microbrews and a wonderful menu featuring local foods; Old St. Francis Theater, which seats up to 150 and lets viewers catch new releases, cult classics, or sporting events while enjoying artisan pizza and ale; and even an on-site brewery where guests can take tours and sample the handmade beers. And after all of that, guests retire for the night to one of the hotel rooms or one of the houses on the property, which can be rented by the night.

But what about the ghosts? Personally, if I were a ghost, this would be the place where I would want to retire. Old St. Francis School is a welcoming sight for the weary traveler, but be aware that you may hear more than your partner snoring in the darkness.

"I'm not saying it's haunted, but it's odd," property manager Jared Smith told the *Eugene Weekly*. He went on to talk about lights that turned on and off by themselves, books being pushed from shelves with no one near them, and even one couple who hurriedly checked out of the nunnery cottage in the middle of the night. "All they said was that the place was haunted."

Smith also spoke about the theater, which was once the gymnasium for the Catholic school, and its unexplained flooding, noises that have no apparent source, and even fire alarms going off randomly.

"It's been an Irish-Catholic school since 1936," he continued. "I'm sure if these walls could speak, there would be some interesting stories."

I got the chance to talk with some of the regulars at the pub and O'Kanes. No one I spoke with seemed at all rattled by the ghosts—which they insisted are definitely there.

"The first time you see something or hear something it's a little scary," one older man told me. "But after that, they just become one of the crowd. They don't bother anyone. And sometimes, when you just want some quiet time, they are better company than the wife!" he added with a husky laugh.

"Lots of us have seen Father Luke," he continued. "He just kinda stands in doorways and looks and then—*poof*—he's off. Just keeping an eye, I suppose. Not sure how he feels about bars and alcohol and such, but he never seems to be mad. Nothing here ever seems to be mad or upset."

I also spoke with a few people who have heard children running and laughing in the theater (the old gymnasium). People often see shadows on the walls or against the screen. Of all the cottages, the nunnery seems to be the one where most people experience paranormal activity. There are reports of footsteps pacing the halls, quiet whispers that seem to be reciting passages from the Bible, and door knobs turning or shaking in the middle of the night. Some people make it the whole night, and others do not. But whether they stay or leave, many people come away with ghost stories about Old St. Francis School.

I had hoped to stay in the nunnery cottage on my visit, but it was unavailable. I did not have experiences anywhere else in the old school but, as I often say, that does not mean that ghosts are not there. I plan on going back, as Bend is one of my favorite towns, and spending a night or two in the nunnery cottage.

Dining, lodging, and two types of spirits at Old St. Francis School in Bend.

Until then, I will rely on what others have told me and on the history. And until I can ask, I will wonder what Father Luke and the nuns think about having a Turkish bath in the middle of the land where the old school sat.

CHAPTER 27

Redmond Hotel

REDMOND

IN 1906, WILLIAM AND FANNY WILSON erected the original Redmond Hotel on the corner of Sixth and Evergreen just a year after their arrival in Redmond from Alaska, where they had amassed a sizeable fortune outfitting and financing prospectors during the Klondike Gold Rush. They immediately felt at home in Redmond and became active members of the community, even organizing a weekly meeting to discuss civic affairs and concerns. They were passionate about the community and felt that if each resident worked together for a common purpose, Redmond would become the go-to town in central Oregon. And the beginning of that vision was the Redmond Hotel.

In June 1927, tragedy struck and a fire of undetermined causes burned the wood-framed structure to the ground. But even this did not deter the Wilsons or destroy their drive and determination, and they immediately set to work replacing the old hotel with a new one, beginning construction on June 27, 1927. And this time they added something—a time capsule. They had it placed in the cornerstone, and community leaders added coins, photographs, newspapers with stories about the hotel fire, and other items pertaining to the Redmond community. Just over a year and $150,000 later, the hotel held its grand opening on July 27, 1928. The event offered tours of the new hotel, a banquet that served 350 people, and a community dance. Early advertisements upon completion of the hotel boasted that the New Redmond Hotel was easily the best lodging east of the Cascade Mountains and that it had the best prices, a mere $1 to $2.50 per day.

The three-story Georgian brick hotel was constructed in the heart of downtown Redmond, and even today, it stands as one of the largest buildings in the business district. The ground floor is divided into the hotel entrance and six storefronts, with the shops separated from each other by rustic brick piers. In 1928, canvas awnings shaded the shop windows, and these were later replaced by a more sensible metal marquee that ran continuously along the front of the building.

The hotel's public places have remained unchanged for the most part over the decades, even though the lobby was previously used as the local chamber of commerce and even a bus station. Once in the lobby, visitors' eyes are drawn to the large rock-faced stone chimneypiece and to the original black-and-white linoleum tiles laid in a checkerboard pattern over the fir flooring. An elevator was installed in the 1940s, and the main floors are now occupied with retail stores, a restaurant complex, and the hotel lobby and office. The upper two stories are home to a laundry facility, chambermaid's storage and supply rooms, 29 sleeping rooms, 28 apartments, a governor's suite, and an executive suite. It seems William and Fanny Wilson's dream has been fulfilled once again.

Klondike Kate, a famous dancer and vaudeville performer during the Klondike Gold Rush who was later known as Kate Rockwell Warner Matson Van Duren, was one of the Wilsons' closest friends and associates since their time in Alaska. Her fame came mostly from her ability to flirt, dance, and keep the hardworking miners happy and inebriated. She never achieved the fame in motion pictures she dreamed of but did achieve celebrity status after her move to Bend. This time, however, her renown came from charitable work instead of dancing. She made friends everywhere she went, and locals knew her as Aunt Kate.

"She was a fund-raising dynamo, able to shake down almost any business or person for a contribution to a social cause," one newspaper article quoted a local man as saying. "During the Great Depression she made gallons and gallons of soup to help out the hobos." Her sense of community and compassion sealed her friendship with the Wilsons.

For years after the opening of the new hotel, William Wilson could be seen like clockwork walking up and down the streets on Monday afternoons ringing his cowbell to let everyone know it was time for the businessman's lunch, where patrons discussed common issues that every city in the nation faced and the future of Redmond. The Wilsons were extremely active in community affairs into the 1940s, and their hotel remained the most popular gathering place in town throughout their ownership of it.

Today the New Redmond Hotel is a major landmark in downtown Redmond, and because of its history and importance to the city, it is listed on the National Register of Historic Places. The lobby is filled with an eclectic collection of antiques and more modern pieces, and guests are invited to relax on the couches in front of the original rock fireplace or head upstairs to their rooms via the original 1940s elevator. Once upstairs, visitors find spacious rooms with furnishings and bathrooms that have evolved with the times, but the original woodwork, high ceilings, and tall windows remind guests that they are in an historical building. Amenities include a gym to work out in, a hot tub to soothe aching muscles, an in-house restaurant, and a central location that enables guests to take a stroll around downtown Redmond at any time.

Two historical markers at the hotel provide information about it. The marker on the inside of the hotel displays information about the Wilsons, while the outdoor marker reads:

Upon completion, the New Redmond Hotel was billed as the finest hotel east of the mountains. Room rates ranged from $1.00 to $2.50 per day. The original Redmond Hotel, a 1906 two-story frame building, burned to the ground in 1927 after a massive fire that also destroyed 2 blocks of the downtown core and twelve businesses. The 43,500 sq. ft. building was designed by Bend architect, Hugh Thompson, and constructed for $150,000.

The New Redmond Hotel is certainly a blast from the past in both its appearance and its history and the many ghost stories. Travelers of all ages enjoy coming to the hotel for rest, relaxation, and the resident spirits. People ages 8–80 have reported paranormal activity for decades; these ghosts seem willing to communicate with anyone, regardless of age, in a friendly manner.

The most reported ghost is that of a young woman who has been seen walking the halls of the guest-room levels. She often appears not to notice anyone around her and will continue walking past and even through people. But every now and then people report that she has stopped and looked directly at them, smiled softly, and then walked away. Witnesses say she does not look sad or seem to be on any particular missions and appears to be content walking the halls. She has been described as slightly transparent but nonetheless clearly seen. She most often wears a light-blue dress, 1920s style, and a feathered hat, and carries what looks like a cloth handkerchief. Those who have seen her firsthand say they are not at all frightened by her, and many, in fact, claim to feel soothed by her presence.

Inside the rooms many guests have been awakened by footsteps near their bed and the overpowering feeling that they are not alone and are being watched. Some have not welcomed this feeling and have packed up in the middle of the night and left. A majority of those I spoke with, however, say they felt uneasy but not frightened and felt intrigued by the invisible presence and did not feel inclined to run.

Some locals say that the female ghost is Fanny Wilson herself, keeping an eye on her guests and watching over the halls of the hotel that she and her husband William built twice. Others say it might be the ghost of Klondike Kate, who was a frequent guest of the Wilsons. Either of them are welcome, locals say, and no one feels the ghosts are there to instill fear.

Many have reported paranormal activity in the lobby after sundown. People have heard disembodied voices, often leaving them wondering who just spoke to them and where they went. Locals who have heard this phenomena tend to simply respond to the voices with a cheerful "Hello" or "Good evening."

"At first I felt weird talking to thin air," a young man who worked at the hotel front desk told me. "But it wasn't thin air really because someone said my name. I spoke back and said hi and asked who they were. I never got an answer, but I think it's a good thing to respond to give them some sort of acknowledgment. I miss the job sometimes, but I miss the ghosts even more."

Whoever is still residing at the New Redmond Hotel is apparently happy to see it still thriving and filled with satisfied guests and visitors. Some people shiver at the word *ghost*, but in reality, such entities are simply the past visiting the present and attempting to communicate with us. When this happens to me I am flattered that they chose me to speak with. So if you visit the Redmond Hotel—and I hope that you will—do not let the ghosts scare you away. They have chosen you for a reason, so just tip your hat, smile, and say hi. That may be the contact that they need, just as we need acknowledgment. Because a smile goes a long way . . . even for a ghost.

Mount Hood—
The Gorge

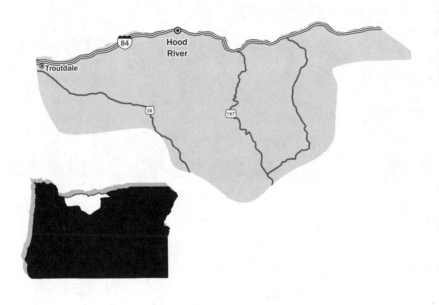

Hood River
  Columbia Gorge Hotel

Troutdale
  Edgefield

Columbia Gorge Hotel
HOOD RIVER

COLUMBIA GORGE HOTEL is one of the state's out-standing resort destinations, built at the onset of the automobile age. It is not only a desirable location but also an enjoyable trip to make in one's newly purchased automobile. The hotel was the vision of Simon Benson, founder of the famous Benson Hotel in Portland (see page 12), and master chef Henry Thiele. Together they envisioned a hotel at the end of the highway, surrounded by lush mountains, breathtaking waterfalls, and the Columbia River, and that is what they achieved.

169

Columbia Gorge Hotel is a lavish Mission-style structure with some definite Italianate features. It was designed by Morris Whitehouse and completed in May 1921. Standing majestically just 1 mile west of the Hood River, it was designed to entice and accommodate travelers along the new Columbia River Highway. The site on which the hotel sits was originally home to a hotel called Wah Gwin Gwin, an American Indian word meaning "rushing waters." The hotel was adjacent to a 280-foot waterfall, which still runs strongly on the grounds today. The Columbia Gorge Hotel is nestled between a high bluff overlooking the Columbia River on the north side and the Columbia River Highway on the south side. Streaming through the middle of the property is Phelps Creek, which forms Wah Gwin Gwin Falls where it cascades into the Columbia River.

Four bridges cross Phelps Creek, and the main one, beautifully constructed of ashlar masonry walls with ornate spiral terminals that frame the masonry lampposts, also serves as the entryway to the hotel. The same masonry techniques are reflected on the terrace and wall built along the edge of the bluff behind the hotel, where visitors can enjoy a wondrous view of Wah Gwin Gwin Falls and the Columbia River. Everything about the Columbia Gorge Hotel is spectacular down to the tiniest detail—and that is what Simon Benson strived for.

Benson did not see the new highway as simply a tedious means of transportation but rather had a broader vision of it as a thoroughfare to the natural beauty of Oregon.

"We have built good roads and invited the world to come and see our beauty spots, but until now we have done nothing toward taking care of them after they arrived," Benson said. "With our new hotel we will, in a measure, take care of this." And, just as Benson envisioned, they arrived in droves.

The hotel had barely opened before word began to spread from coast to coast and country to country; it had gained an international reputation without even trying. It was a hotel fit for a king, and definitely for the royalty of the United States, and the Columbia Gorge Hotel quickly became known as "The Waldorf of the West." Among its famous guests were Presidents Roosevelt and Coolidge, along with Hollywood luminaries Clara Bow, Shirley Temple, Myrna Loy, Jane Powell, and silent film sex symbol Rudolph Valentino (and, in more recent years, Burt Reynolds, Kevin Costner, and Olivia Newton-John). Many other hotels of the era offered theaters with films featuring favorite movie stars, but the Columbia Gorge Hotel offered the movie stars themselves.

During the Great Depression, however, the hotel fell upon hard times along with the rest of the nation. It was subsequently foreclosed upon and purchased by the Neighbors of Woodcraft, who turned it into a retirement home, and it remained as such for 25 years. Then, in 1978, the Columbia Gorge Hotel was sold to a corporation that shared Simon Benson's vision of a grand hotel, and after $1 million in renovations, the 42-room hotel reopened in September 1979.

In 2009, the monumental hotel once again closed its doors due to foreclosure, and in October of that year it was purchased by Vijay Patel's A-1 Hospitality Group for $4.6 million. Between 2009 and 2012, the hotel underwent a major renovation and, today, has been restored to its original luxury and is recognized as one of the Historic Hotels of America by the National Trust for Historic Preservation.

Stories of specific ghosts have been told and retold over the years at the Columbia Gorge Hotel, and for many years management did all they could to discourage retelling of such accounts, especially to the public. When haunted hotels became more fashionable in the 1980s, however, they began to document each report and keep a running log, much like Heceta Head Lighthouse (see page 93), and these efforts continue to this day.

Paranormal activity seemed to increase tenfold during the 1978 renovation. One of the first indications that something supernatural was wandering the halls of the hotel was when each and every wall sconce in the third floor hallway was turned completely upside down. The honeymoon suite on the floor had just been reopened following the renovation, but no guests were staying in it at the time. It wasn't that all the sconces inexplicably became loose and fell upside down—they had been deliberately remounted. Restoring them to their proper positions was quite the task for the maintenance worker, and it took him the rest of his shift.

Many of the accounts of ghostly activity at the hotel, in fact, appear to be associated with the honeymoon suite near the hotel tower. A couple sitting in the suite on their wedding night report seeing a young woman emerge from the bathroom, look directly at them, and then suddenly disappear. Another guest reported seeing, as she crossed the parking lot, a dark-haired young woman in a formal white dress leaping from the hotel tower. The woman did not land on the pavement but disappeared about halfway down during the fall.

A story that has been told for many years is that of a young bride who murdered her new husband in the third-floor honeymoon suite in the 1930s. Realizing what she had done and understanding the consequences for her heat-of-passion crime, she felt she had no other choice than to jump from the window, ending her life as she landed in the parking lot. I have not been able to verify this murder-suicide, but the story has been shared for many years with little deviation from the original accounts.

The third floor in general seems to be a paranormal hot spot within the hotel. Housekeeping staff has reported the water in sinks turning on as they work, guests have claimed to see television sets going off and on before their eyes, fires have started by themselves in the fireplaces, and empty rooms have had heavy furniture barricading the doors from the inside. Other accounts describe people feeling hands on their shoulders or faces, sensing tugs on clothing, and hearing whispers in their ears. There have not been any reports of guests getting hurt during any of these occurrences, but a fair number have simply packed up their suitcases and checked out before the sun came up, not wanting to spend another moment in the room wondering what the ghosts would do or say next.

Some speculate that many of the ghosts were former residents of the nursing home, who passed away in their rooms and decided to remain in the lavish building. One particular nursing home resident is, in fact, said to have often barricaded her door to prevent nursing staff from entering and invading her privacy. Having worked in nursing and in care facilities myself, I am familiar with the spirits of residents who choose to remain or visit and have experienced it many times over the years, so I find these reports to be quite plausible.

As much as I would have liked to, I did not see or hear anything when I walked down the third floor hallway. My surroundings looked and sounded completely normal for a slower

Visitors to the Columbia Gorge Hotel today can enjoy the same luxury as Rudolph Valentino and Clara Bow did.

weekday, but I did have the strong sense that I was being watched or followed or both, which was not as frightening as it was frustrating. It always makes me uneasy to know something is near but not be able to see it, but I also did not feel threatened or the need to run screaming from the area. I wandered a bit longer and, as I left, thanked whoever was there for their company.

With such an eclectic history, I have no doubt that the Columbia Gorge Hotel is indeed haunted. It has been associated with the local American Indians, has been a destination for presidents and movie stars, has been a nursing home, and has come full circle to the wondrous hotel it began as under the passionate eye of Simon Benson. Undoubtedly even more stories fall in between those transitions. I could have spent a week there and not taken in everything there was to see and experience, but the time I did spend there was something I will never forget. I fully intend to return and, hopefully, embark on a night in the honeymoon suite.

The drive to the Columbia Gorge Hotel is something you can only imagine until you see it firsthand, and once you are there you will feel as though you have discovered your own personal paradise. Each aged piece of wood, each tile, each vintage photograph and painting exudes history and days long gone, yet they are still close enough that you can reach out and touch them and the times for which they are a gateway. And I would conclude that these are precisely the reasons why the ghosts have chosen to stay at the hotel: for its beauty, its strength, its persistence, its breathtaking surroundings. I certainly cannot wait until I am able to go back and spend enough time to explore each and every nook and cranny.

At the end of the highway sits the Columbia Gorge Hotel, and for some it was literally the end of the road. But it does not appear as though they left when their journeys were over—and I can assure you that they will be waiting to say hello when you arrive.

CHAPTER 29

Edgefield

TROUTDALE

TODAY, VISITORS TO EDGEFIELD bed-and-breakfast and hostel will find quaint and comfortable rooms and hostel accommodations with bunk beds, four taste-tempting restaurants, six bars and pubs, a winery tasting room, and a golf course. Other amenities include a salon and spa, a theater, live music in many of the establishment's venues, and even an art gallery. But Edgefield was not always so welcoming and glamorous for those who rested their heads there, as it was once Multnomah County's poorhouse, a residence for disturbed children, and a tuberculosis ward. Many believe that the spirits of former residents continue to haunt the place where they spent so many troubled years.

"We are not writing . . . a history of the poorfarm," Harry C. Evens wrote in 1926 in the introduction of *The American Poorfarm and its Inmates*. "We hope we are writing its obituary."

In 1868, Oregon's first poorhouse opened in Portland. It was named Hillside Farm and rested on 160 acres of Oregon greenery at the site that is now Washington Park. It was not long, however, before Hillside Farm closed its doors due to deplorable conditions, and the residents were shuffled to the new location in Troutdale. Multnomah County Poor Farm was the largest county-funded institution in Oregon, and 211 former residents of Hillside Farm became its first residents. Here, they were self-sufficient, working on the farm, in the laundry facilities and kitchen, and even in a hospital wing and a jail.

Men, women, and children from every walk of life assembled as one big family beneath the roof of the poorhouse: sea captains, schoolteachers, musicians, writers, artists, nurses, housewives, loggers, fishermen, former slaves, and former slave owners alike. Every ethnic group was represented, among them Americans, Germans, Jews, Japanese, Chinese, and African Americans. And nearly each religion could be found there, including Catholics, Protestants, Baptists, Buddhists, and Muslims. Even the nephew of the famed Confederate General Stonewall Jackson not only called the poorhouse home but lived past the age of 100 while there. It was an eclectic group to be sure, but one thing bound them together and that was the need for a hand up in life. No one, it seemed, was immune to the vicissitudes of fortune.

A few years later, when the Great Depression overtook many families, the population of the poor farm ballooned to more than 600. With little room to spare to house double the number of residents, rooms such as closets and pantries were converted to sleeping quarters and equipped with makeshift beds to accommodate the new arrivals. Residents became close in these conditions, and together they made the best of a drastic situation and converted the basement to a belowground marketplace for the many talented individuals who lived upstairs. Booths were built, and the residents displayed their wares and crafts and baked goods to eager Portland customers.

By 1934, an infirmary was added to care for aging residents, and, in 1935, the population hit its peak with 614 inhabitants. When the 1940s rolled around, Americans went back to work at jobs created by World War II, and the population of the poorhouse declined drastically. Those who did remain were generally old or too incapacitated to leave, so the poor farm became more of a nursing home and rehabilitation facility, but farming operations nonetheless continued fruitfully through the 1960s.

In 1947, the name of the poorhouse was officially changed to the Multnomah County Home and Farm. A few new additions included a physician's duplex on the grounds, a sunporch, a modern sprinkler system, and an incinerator.

In the latter part of the 1950s, the farming operation ceased completely and the name of the facility was once again changed, this time to Edgefield Manor, and it was operated as a tuberculosis hospital. In 1964, part of the site, now known as Edgefield Lodge, was used to house emotionally disturbed children, with the main building remaining a nursing home and retaining the name Edgefield Manor. Later the same year the entire complex was renamed Edgefield Center by the county's commissioners, but to people in Troutdale and surrounding areas, it thereafter remained Edgefield Manor.

As the 1970s began, Edgefield Manor saw a drastic decline in incoming patients and residents of the nursing home. More affordable nursing care options, long-term care facilities, and in-home health-care options were becoming more popular. With the resident population shrinking rapidly and the building upkeep and repairs becoming more complex and expensive, county officials decided to close the doors to Edgefield once and for all. In 1982, the last of the Edgefield patients were successfully relocated and the old building was boarded up and locked down.

During the 1980s, violent weather and vandals had their way with the property, wreaking havoc on every wall and window they could get to. Pipes were broken, sending water gushing everywhere throughout the old building, windows were smashed, graffiti became the only visible paint, and anything that could be carried was stolen and carted away. The facility that kept those in need safe for so many years was now a dangerous liability for the Troutdale community.

In 1985, the county commissioners decided to demolish all of the buildings except for the jail, hoping they would better be able to market the property to prospective buyers without the rotting structures. But the members of Troutdale Historical Society strongly opposed this move, and, in 1986, they challenged the decision to destroy the buildings, calling it a "foul and unjust fate." Thus began a five-year battle to save Edgefield Manor, and one in which the historical society eventually claimed victory over county officials. They were then faced with another issue—who would want to buy an old poor farm/nursing home/tuberculosis hospital/home for emotionally disturbed children? There were no takers in Oregon, and even a listing with a New York auction house yielded no interest. It appeared as if their fight might have been in vain.

This is where two familiar brothers from Oregon—Brian and Mike McMenamin—entered the picture. The McMenamin

brothers are legendary in Oregon for buying old historical buildings and transforming them into trendy hotels, restaurants, bars
and pubs, music venues, and theaters, and they worked their
magic on Edgefield Manor. (Other McMenamin locations in this
book include the White Eagle Saloon in Portland, on page 62,
and Old St. Francis School in Bend, on page 156.)

In 1990 the Edgefield Winery was born and subsequently
Edgefield Manor's wine-tasting room. The winery produces
red, white, sparkling, and dessert wines, and even a Poor Farm
Pinot gris that pays tribute to the humble beginnings of Edgefield Manor.

In 1991, the site welcomed a brewery, the Power Station
Pub, a movie theater, and eight guest rooms. With much of
the McMenamins' borrowed money spent on giving new life
to Edgefield Manor, little was spent on advertising, but it was
not long before word of mouth began to spread and people
were traveling quite a distance to visit the site. The initial success of Edgefield allowed the brothers to move forward with
more improvements, such as adding more hotel rooms in the
main lodge, bars and pubs, fine-dining restaurants, and even
an events center. They landscaped with breathtaking gardens,
added local artisan shops, offered concerts by the likes of B. B.
King and Ringo Starr, and even installed a golf course. And,
in the process, each and every building and outbuilding of the
original Edgefield Manor was saved. Even the incinerator was
given new life as a bar called the Little Red Shed. Nothing was
unimportant, and nothing was left behind.

Even as historic Edgefield Manor has been preserved, many
people believe that the ghosts of many former inhabitants still
reside at the site. Deaths were not uncommon in poorhouses,
homes for the emotionally ill, or tuberculosis facilities, and it
is believed that many of those who died there were buried in
unmarked graves on the property.

Of all the places I have visited during the writing of this book, Edgefield Manor has, by far, the most ghost stories and accounts of paranormal activity. That did not surprise me, as all of the original buildings still exist—their history never left.

Room 215 is a common location for paranormal activity in the hotel. It is said that when the McMenamins purchased the property and began cleanup, this room, more so than any other at the site, was covered with cult symbols and graffiti. The ghost that purportedly haunts this room is not a man or a woman or a child, however; it is a dog. Many guests have reported that a large, transparent dog pushes its nose into their faces as they sleep and continues to do so until they awaken. Another routine report of those staying in the hotel is that of someone gripping their ankles during the night.

One employee related to me a feeling of being strapped down to a bed, something that was probably a fairly common occurrence when the place served as a tuberculosis hospital and a home for the emotionally ill. Guests have also reported that their belongings had been moved or scattered throughout the room while they were at dinner or other activities.

People have seen a woman wearing white who seems to enjoy peering into first floor windows at night, startling guests and employees. People often see her with a young boy walking through the parking lot.

"They just look and walk," one frequent guest told me. "They walk until they fade into nothing, like fog."

What was once the hospital is now the area over the winery, and there many have reported suddenly feeling overcome with grief. Some have even begun to cry openly for no reason. This area has more than one ghost, according to those who have been there on more than a few occasions. They include the spirit of a nurse who has been seen walking the hallways, day and night; a young girl who many believe is the old poor farm administrator's daughter, who passed away during his tenure; and a young

African American man in tattered clothing. People I spoke with said these ghosts do not speak and do not bother anyone, but that they will stop to look at the living from time to time before they disappear.

There have been stories that a young woman was murdered in one of the guest rooms, and many people, especially men, did not like the feeling they got when they entered. I was not able to verify a murder, but old death records from a poor farm likely disappear into history, along with the residents.

A glimpse of the winery at Edgefield.

Some simply cannot handle the feeling of being in a room with a ghost, and quite a few guests have left Edgefield abruptly during the night. One woman I corresponded with said that as soon as she and her husband entered their room she was overcome first with anxiety and then full-blown panic. In tears, she begged her husband to leave the hotel and take her home, three hours away.

"He's a good guy, he took me home," she wrote to me. "I was having full-blown panic attacks, and it wasn't stopping. I didn't feel like anything was going to hurt me. I had just never experienced anything like that before. I know there was someone I couldn't see in the room looking at us. But I faced my fears. And now we go back every year. . . . I still don't sleep much, but I'm not crying like a baby to go home in the middle of the night anymore."

Guests have phoned the front desk to ask if there was a day-care facility on the site, not because they had children but because they had heard crying and moaning through the walls. There is no day care at Edgefield, and one explanation may be that one of the hotel wings was, long ago, the infirmary.

When I visited Edgefield, I could feel a thickness in the air and a sense of sadness. I was not overwhelmed as many have been, but the feeling caught me a bit off guard. As I had dinner with a friend, I felt a cold spot next to me twice. I checked and double-checked that no air vents were running or windows opened and confirmed that there were not. Sometimes, however, these things have no rational explanation.

Edgefield is one of those rare locations that has something for everyone, including vintage-style guest rooms, restaurants and bars, a brewery, a winery, a theater showing new-release films and sporting events live on the big screen, a salon and spa that will leave you feeling refreshed and pampered, a golf course, an art gallery, beautiful gardens, and Oregon scenery. And, for the more adventurous, the haunted history and the ghosts.

Eastern Oregon

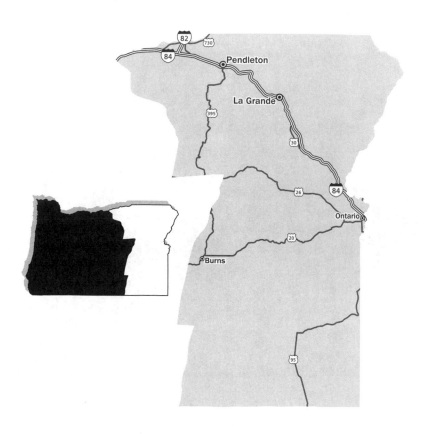

Burns
  Ye Olde Castle Restaurant

Ontario
  Malheur Butte

Pendleton
  Pioneer Park

CHAPTER 30

Malheur Butte
ONTARIO

WITH AN EARTHLY HISTORY that spans 15 million to 20 million years, it is no wonder people believe that strange beings, from ghosts and witches to sprites and fairies, exist on Malheur Butte. This once-active volcano does not lack paranormal phenomena.

Malheur Butte's volcano is now extinct, but millions of years ago it was a ferocious threat to the area between northern Washington and northern California, spewing forth floods of lava that covered thousands of square miles in a series of volcanic eruptions. The lava dammed streams and created lakes and swamps that may have remained in existence for millions of years before filling with sediment. The Snake River contained many such lakes, and many geologists believe that Lake Idaho covered most of eastern Oregon more than 2 million years ago. Sediment that at one time covered Malheur Butte was deposited in Lake Idaho, and over the span of a few million years, the Malheur River ebbed and slowly exposed the ancient butte we see today.

While Malheur Butte's volcano has been inactive for millions of years, the area is still alive with geothermal activity in the form of amazing hot springs. Oregon Trail Mushroom Farm employs the geothermal energy at its processing plant in Vale, and other companies in the area also aspire to put the unique energy source to practical uses.

The rock that makes up the point of the butte and resembles a bear head is more than 300 feet higher than the surrounding plains, and the peak of the rock is about 2,600 feet above sea level. It is easily the most distinctive natural landmark in the Ontario area.

Malheur Butte's name is most likely taken from the Malheur River. The word *Malheur* is derived from the French words *mal*, meaning "bad," and *heur*, meaning "hour." The name was explained by Peter Skene Ogden, a native of Quebec, Canada, in his 1826 journals. Ogden was a fur trader traveling with French-Canadian hunters and wrote that the Malheur River acquired its name because supplies and furs that had been hidden in the rocky vicinity were stolen by American Indians.

Journals of many early travelers along the Oregon trail mention the Malheur River and the hot spring in which they could bathe and wash the dirt from their clothing and cooking utensils. It was an area favored by trappers, abundant with beavers. Early journals indicate that a temporary trading post was eventually built, along with a small cabin and a barn near the hot springs. The more people came or passed through, the more the stories of ghosts and other supernatural beings grew.

Many paranormal researchers feel certain conditions are prime for hauntings and other supernatural activity. These include water, which is said to be a type of conductor used to communicate from one realm to another, various forms of natural energy, and many types of stone or rock, which may act as a magnetic tape that retain a record of events and human or non-human energy within their cores. If there is any truth to this, then it would stand to reason that Malheur Butte would be an impeccable location to witness and experience the paranormal, as it has all of these factors in abundance.

It is not just ghosts, however, that are said to roam Malheur Butte. Some say witches travel to the rock to engage in their covens and rituals, and many tell stories of imps, sprites, or fairies, animal spirits, shadow people, and strange cloud-like figures. If any location possessed all aspects of the paranormal, it would certainly be Malheur Butte.

I have visited Malheur Butte many times over the years. The feeling of standing on a site that existed before man is awe-inspiring and thought-provoking, and imagining the black rock as the molten lava it once was sparks the imagination to a scene it may never have conceived before. Our ability to research this site completely is limited, as no written accounts date back millions of years, and so we are left to fill in those gaps with our imaginations.

Most of my visits have been during the summer, when the weather is hot and the sun beats down in nearly visible rays. Come wintertime, the roads can be quite slippery and hazardous due to snow and ice, but I have made that trip off US 20 then as well. I have always found it interesting that even during the winter people are making the same trip as me, taking pictures of the butte and perhaps seeking something a little more than scenery.

Legend says that as far back as a century ago witches met in secret to perform rituals and cast spells. Some Ontario locals say that either witches or their ghosts carry on that tradition to this day, and you can regularly see them behind the rocks.

"I've been here a long time . . . a long time," an older resident of nearby Vale, Oregon, told me. "And I've seen some things that I expect most folks read about in books. . . . The witches? I've heard about the witches since I was a boy, and I was always told not to go to the butte after dark. So of course I did! Can't say I'm positive I saw witches, but more than once I've seen robes . . . long robes that flap in the wind, more than one. Sometimes women laughing, but not in a funny way . . . more of a serious kind of laugh. I don't know. I know each time I left pretty fast! I think there are witches, either ghosts of witches or living witches. I don't have the intention to interrupt them, either."

Others have seen what they call sprites or fairies, which they often describe as shadows about the size of a small dog darting from rock to rock. When the sun sets, these shadows take on a glowing effect, according to those I spoke with who have witnessed the phenomena. No one was fearful, but they did feel uneasy, and many complained about feeling suddenly nauseated. I looked at a few pictures that locals showed me of the fairies, but to me they resembled bugs reflecting off the flash of a camera. I could be wrong—I have never seen anything I thought might be a fairy during my trips to Malheur Butte or anywhere else, so I have nothing to use as a point of reference.

A few visitors have reportedly been chased to the safety of their cars by something they could not see. They could hear a distinctive growling sound and footsteps following them as they ran. One woman who claims this happened to her on a November evening a few years ago said she did take the chance of looking over her shoulder to see what was pursuing her.

"It wasn't very big, maybe the size of a small dog, a Chihuahua maybe," she told me. "Now I am not one who scares very easily. I have seen ghosts and have even done a few investigations for friends who feel their houses are haunted. But this didn't feel like Casper to me. I didn't feel like my life was in danger or anything like that, but I sure did feel like it wanted me out of there immediately! I didn't sleep for a few days, trying to figure it all out. All I could come up with was that I am not going back there alone at night anymore!"

Others have experienced the same foot pursuit, which, to me, lent some reliability to this woman's statement.

The ghosts bring people interested in the paranormal to Malheur Butte and the areas around it. Perhaps because the histories of the many trappers and hunters, the missionaries, the American Indians, and the homesteaders who lived and died there can be validated. These were the people who traveled the Oregon Trail through rain and snow and sweltering heat to make a living and seek new homes for themselves and their families, the people who wrote the history of Oregon.

With others visiting as well, I had difficulty recording potential EVPs during one of my visits to the site. Even with other tourists in the distance and the breeze that often catches you off guard on the hill, however, I did manage to record one voice and one word: "Hello." Ordinarily I would dismiss anything that was accompanied by ambient sounds and voices, no matter how far away they were, but this voice seemed to drown out the background sounds. It was the voice of a male, very deep and very loud, as though the source was speaking directly into the built-in microphone of my digital recorder, but it was also strong, friendly, and welcoming. Had I known at the time that I had received this greeting, I would have stayed much longer than I did. But when I find myself traveling US 20, I make a point to stop at the butte and say my own hello.

The older man I spoke to about the witches summed up Malheur Butte for me: "You know, it's been there for millions of years. Who am I to say I know all of its secrets or the remnants that were left behind when everything else died away. Sometimes life's mysteries are supposed to stay that way. And I reckon that old butte knows more than any of us."

CHAPTER 31

Pioneer Park

PENDLETON

PIONEER PARK IN PENDLETON is the oldest park in the area and is well known for its large, castle-like play structure. Children love climbing on it and playing on the slides, swings, and sand around it while parents watch from beneath the many shade trees. It is everything a children's park should be—at first glance. But when you look a bit closer, you notice a few things that just don't seem to belong in a park filled with laughing children, babies in strollers, and romping puppies. Here and there, scattered about the perfectly manicured lawns, are headstones marking the burial sites of men, women, and children who called Pendleton home as long as a century ago. Local residents are used to this sight, but visitors sometimes do a double take.

Back in the 1870s, the land on which Pioneer Park sits today was donated to the community by residents Moses and Aura Goodwin for use as a cemetery. It became known as Pendleton Cemetery and accepted burials for more than 20 years. Upkeep was not as regular as one might expect for a final resting place; grass and invasive species covered the plots, and the headstones fell into tragic disrepair, some disappearing completely.

In 1891, Olney Cemetery opened on the south side of town and most of those buried at Pendleton Cemetery were transferred to the new site with the old one transformed into a park. But because permission of a surviving family member was needed to relocate a gravesite, those buried there without next of kin to give their endorsement could not be moved and remain in Pioneer Park to this day. Cemetery records show that 13 known gravesites are left in Pioneer Park, and probably more remain to be discovered.

Gravesites at Pioneer Park include those of Mr. and Mrs. L. L. Lewis, who died on August 1, 1878, only days after all three of their children, who died on July 28. There are no records of what claimed the lives of an entire family, and even in a time when today's common illnesses were fatal, it would be unusual that three children would succumb to an illness on the same day and then the parents just days later and on the same date. Anything is possible, of course, but not always probable.

A more famous gravesite belongs to George Augustus LaDow, a member of the Minnesota House of Representatives from 1868 until 1869 and the Oregon State House of Representatives from 1872 until 1874. He shares a headstone in Pioneer Park with his wife, Vicky, and is still regarded as a local celebrity.

Many graves were not adorned with markers, and those still remain beneath the surface of Pioneer Park. During the 19th century, many simply could not afford headstones, leaving no visible sign of their presence in the cemetery. Many headstones have also decayed. Some say the ghosts of those who have remained unidentified haunt the park today, begging to be heard.

"I remember when the playground was being constructed," Diane LaSarge of the Oregon Commission on Historic Cemeteries told the *East Oregonian* newspaper in 2003. "They were so sure that they knew where all the graves were. Then, when they were putting the walkway in around the playground, they found three new graves that they hadn't known about."

For some, the ghosts were brought to mind again on October 6, 2012, just after midnight, when a suspicious fire broke out at the park and reduced the castle play structure to ashes. The cause of the fire remains unknown, and some still whisper that those forgotten beneath the playground were imploring the community to look for them.

"The castle isn't a little structure," a young woman, who claimed to be psychic, told me about her theories on the fire and on the ghosts in general. "It must have taken some time to get that fire going. But it still hasn't been determined how it started, and there is still a reward for information. I won't go so far as to say the spirits caused it, but I won't say they didn't either. There are so many people buried here that haven't been found. I can see them and hear them. They aren't angry, just sad and lost. But you don't have to have the gift to feel them, and almost everyone feels them."

As it turned out, she was correct about residents feeling the ghosts around them. There were very few people I spoke with who did not admit to the sensation of being watched while in the park. Some had even heard footsteps behind them as they traveled along the footpath or claimed to have heard whispers in their ears.

"I've only lived here a few years," one young mother who stood by watching her daughter play told me. "But I get creeped out here, especially in the evening. It's just weird to me that there are headstones right in the middle of a park. I pay my respects every time we come here, but it just doesn't seem like enough. I believe there are ghosts here. I get chills on hot days to the point the hair on my arms stands up, and I always feel like I'm being watched. I thought I saw something once, like a whitish figure. It was just a second or two. I spent a long time trying to explain it away. I never did."

What was most interesting about my conversation with this woman was that when I played my recording of it to transcribe it for this book I heard a whisper speaking over us, saying, "Hey . . . hey . . . hey!" It was a male voice, and there had been no men around us. I believe that voice to be that of someone trying to gain the attention of the living.

I stayed in the park, listening and watching, until the sun began to sink over a hill. I heard nothing at that time nor did I see anything, but I did have the feeling of being watched that I had heard so many people speak about during the day. I fully expected more than once to turn around to see someone stand-ing behind me.

When I left the park, I found myself aware and cautious of where I stepped; I was told at an early age that stepping on a grave was disrespectful to the dead, and I still believe that to be true. But when you are walking through a park with so many graves that have never been located, it is hard to determine where to step and where not to step. I knew as I left that I was probably not the only person in the area to have contended with that dilemma. As I write this, I am reminded of a passage from the Gospel of Luke: "Woe to you! For you are like unmarked graves, and people walk over them without knowing it."

I do not believe there is anything to be afraid of at Pioneer Park or that anything there means harm to anyone. It is, at the same time, a place of great joy for the children who enjoy the playground, and a place of great sadness for those who have been lost beneath the earth. But I hold out hope that one day the missing will be found and given a proper resting place. Until then, enjoy their company and pay your respects to those who may feel lost and are reaching out with respect to you.

CHAPTER 32

Ye Olde Castle Restaurant

BURNS

TO PEOPLE FROM LARGER CITIES, Burns often seems like a step back in time, and it can cause a bit of culture shock. A truly rustic western town with two-lane main streets, plenty of brick and stone buildings, and just 3,000 inhabitants, Burns takes great pride in its history, as is apparent in galleries featuring American Indian history, rodeo lore, and western art. Located in Harney County, the largest county by area in Oregon, Burns and the nearby city of Hines are home to 60% of the county's population, making it one of the most sparsely populated counties in the nation.

Burns was named for the Scottish poet Robert Burns when George McGowen, a local shopkeeper, stood steadfast against the town being named after Peter Stenger, who had established the community's post office. He contended that if the town were named after Stenger, it would be known as "the Stenger town where they got stung" and insisted that it instead be named after Burns, who he called the "poet of the people." Perhaps the beginning stanza of "Composed in Spring" convinced McGowen that Burns was speaking of the little town in eastern Oregon:

> *Again rejoicing Nature sees*
> *Her robe assume its vernal hues:*
> *Her leafy looks wave in the breeze,*
> *All freshly steep'd in morning dews.*

There is no more accurate description for this little town that has been preserved in time. Visitors will not find shopping malls or multiscreen theaters, but they will discover many small shops and just as many restaurants; in a town filled with cattle ranchers, ranch hands, and timber workers, there must be a good hot meal at the end of the day, even if it is not at home. One restaurant that caters to local working men and women is Ye Olde Castle—and it is also said that it caters to a female ghost as well.

Ye Olde Castle is an odd combination restaurant and antique emporium, and many people love the collection of objects displayed as much as they do the restaurant. It is not the prettiest eatery in town, but it is certainly the most unique, and quite possibly the most haunted.

Though not much is known about the history of the building, it dates back to the mid-to-late 1800s, when it was a private home, and sits less than 2 miles from three cemeteries—the Burns Cemetery, the Paiute Cemetery, and the Burns Paiute Cemetery. Located on West Monroe Street, Ye Olde Castle is a good-sized restaurant that can seat up to 120 people. Locals love the 1950s-style home cooking, and tourists cannot resist the allure of the odd-looking building, the collection of antique toys and bicycles, and the ghost stories.

The restaurant has not changed much over the years and retains its retro feel with shag-carpeted restrooms and old, long-used booths. It features basic breakfast and lunch fare that is as good as grandma used to make, especially the pies that will leave your mouth watering for more. While you are waiting for your meal, you will be entertained by the antique bicycles, toys, paintings, and everything in between. There is no skimping on flavor or the past.

While people claim to have seen more than one ghost in Ye Olde Castle, the one reported most often is a younger woman in a period blue dress. Many say she was a resident of the building when it was a private residence and passed away there, while others say she was the friend of a previous owner whose life was cut short by cancer. Whoever she is, she is reported to have a motherly and compassionate presence, and she has left witnesses scratching their heads over her identity for decades.

Usually witnesses see the woman in blue from the corner of their eye and then as a full-bodied apparition when they turn to look at her, after which she makes eye contact and then quickly disappears. But those who have seen the azure apparition say that even though she disappears, her presence is still felt strongly in the room, as though she remains incognito, watching the customers and staff and their goings-on. People see her more often when workers are repairing or painting the building, which theory says is common for ghosts who have an emotional attachment to a location; they have remained as they were when they died and expect their homes to remain the same as well. Some ghosts may not comprehend that they are deceased and do not understand why strangers are changing their homes.

Whatever the cause in the case of Ye Olde Castle, the woman in blue does not seem to mind being seen. She seems to genuinely care about what happens in the restaurant and appears to have a motherly affection for those who dine and work there.

"There are so many different stories that they tend to get muddled, so it's hard to figure out who exactly she might be," the wife of a local rancher told me. "I have seen her twice over the course of about 10 years, and she looks very sweet, maybe in her 30s, hair up with a long pale blue dress. She always seems to be smiling. I don't know if I have actually seen her smile or if I just got the feeling she was smiling. But the few times I have seen her, I know I have smiled back before she is gone again. . . . Personally, I think she lived here at one time before this was a restaurant. A lot of people died pretty young in the 1800s, so that is my guess and my feeling. Maybe she is confused by the restaurant or maybe she likes the cooking here because it's old-school homestyle food. Or maybe the antiques. Seems to me there is something that brings back memories for her or makes her feel at home. I am probably overanalyzing it, but that's just the feeling I get. She's a sweet girl who likes to pop in and say hi to people. Nothing wrong with that."

I enjoyed my conversation with this woman and did not feel that she was overanalyzing the ghost situation. I have always said that the best tool anyone interested in the paranormal can have is their gut instinct, and the woman I spoke with in the restaurant put hers to great use.

I also spoke to a young man who often drove the 100-plus miles from Ontario to Burns just to enjoy his favorite breakfast at Ye Olde Castle and to hopefully catch another glimpse of his favorite ghost, the lady in blue. He had quite a different theory about the ghost, and about ghosts in general.

"Just to be clear, I'm not a scientist, I'm not a ghost hunter, I just like to think outside the box and look at all possible angles," he clarified for me. "I saw her once, the lady ghost here. It was quick, but I did see what I thought to be a curious look to her, like she was surprised to see me. And I thought, 'What if she isn't a ghost, what if I am the ghost to her?' There are more and more things being written about parallel universes, times running parallel to ours, and that made me think. It could explain a lot. What if the past never dies, and the future is happening at the same time as the present and the past? And what if it is all right here in front of us, existing simultaneously? Science doesn't really want to waste their time on paranormal claims, so we kind of have to play with the theories by ourselves. We can't see all the dimensions in time. Our eyes are two-dimensional and that is how we see. It's our brain that tells our eyes that we are seeing three dimensions. And, if you have ever listened to Carl Sagan, he talks about four dimensions. If we can only see two dimensions, we are missing out on a lot!"

He had my attention from the moment he opened his mouth to speak, and he echoed many of the things I have theorized about for many years. It was refreshing to see a new generation considering the more hidden options of the paranormal. I urged him to continue.

"Maybe she gets a glimpse of us just like we get that glimpse of her. Maybe she thinks she is seeing ghosts. They say she comes around more often when they make changes here. I would get upset too if I saw a bunch of ghosts painting my house!" he laughed. "I may be way off base here . . . but what if I'm not?"

In all honesty, it made my day to hear someone other than myself and my team members thinking about this. Either way, whether it is a ghost from the past who has long since died or a glimpse of a parallel dimension, it is still paranormal and would be further validation that the past does not die.

As I discovered, the lady in blue is not the only paranormal phenomena that people have experienced at Ye Olde Castle. I spoke with a few locals who claim they have heard the sounds of American Indian drums, first at a distance and then close enough that they could be in the same room. There was never a visual aspect to this phenomena, but it did bring to mind for those who experienced it the long history of the Paiute Indians in Burns, where even today the Burns Paiute Reservation exists mere miles away and is home to more than 300 members of the tribe. Could it be that tribe members from days gone by still return to their home in Burns?

I finished my breakfast and had another cup of coffee as I admired the hundreds of antiques that adorned the restaurant. I wondered if one of the pieces could have belonged to the lady in blue. I did not see her, but the people I spoke with brought her to life for me and painted a very loving picture of a beautiful young woman who watched over people in the establishment. I could have sat there all day and hoped for a chance to see her, but I knew that instead each time I was even remotely near the town of Burns I would stop at Ye Olde Castle Restaurant to enjoy the home cooking, the antiques, the wonderful local people, and, hopefully, to catch a glimpse of the kindly woman in blue.

Oregon
Haunted
Road Trip
Travel Guide

AMERICA'S
HAUNTED ROAD TRIP

Visiting Haunted Sites

THE CHAPTERS AND LOCATIONS in this book have been divided into seven geographical areas: the Greater Portland Area, the Willamette Valley, the Oregon Coast, Southern Oregon, Central Oregon, Mount Hood-The Gorge, and Eastern Oregon. I visited each of the locations and offered my account of each visit as well as the history of each site. Oregon has a number of locations that are considered the most haunted in the nation, and I am certain that a visit to any of them will not disappoint. Updated travel information can also be found at the dedicated *Ghosthunting Oregon* blog (**ghosthuntingoregon.blogspot.com**).

OREGON

Oregon is almost 100,000 square miles in area and home to nearly 4 million people, making it the 9th largest US state in area and the 27th largest in population. Set in the Pacific Northwest, it borders the massive Pacific Ocean on the west, Washington on the north, California on the south, Idaho on the east, and Nevada on the southeast. Oregon was home to many American Indian tribes before settlers, trappers, and explorers claimed the area as their own. With their help, the Oregon Territory was formed in 1848, and on February 14, 1859, Oregon became the 33rd state of the Union.

GREATER PORTLAND AREA

Greater Portland sits just 70 miles from the Pacific Ocean and is Oregon's most metropolitan area. Downtown Portland extends along the banks of the Willamette River, which divides the city into east and west sections before detouring to the northwest to

join the Columbia River. The Columbia forms the natural bound-
ary between Oregon and Washington and divides Portland from
Vancouver, Washington. Currently dormant but potentially active
volcano Mount Hood lies to the east, and you can see the active
volcano Mount St. Helens from higher Portland elevations.

Bagdad Theatre 503-249-7474
3702 SE Hawthorn, Portland, OR 97214
mcmenamins.com/219-bagdad-theater-pub-home
This theater, built in 1927 and now owned by the McMenamin brothers, has a
haunted history. You may visit for a tour or catch a movie, but be prepared to encounter the stagehand who hanged himself behind the curtain or the male ghost
who lingers at the site, hoping, perhaps, for his final role on the Bagdad stage.
   Hours: Due to a varied schedule, please call or visit the website for more
information.

Benson Hotel 503-228-2000
309 SW Broadway, Portland, OR 97205
coasthotels.com/hotels/oregon/portland/the-benson-hotel
This extravagant 1912 hotel is considered one of the most haunted in the Portland
area. Many say guests can expect to see long-deceased owner Simon Benson
himself in the hotel as well as other paranormal phenomena, such as cold spots
and disembodied voices.

Cathedral Park 503-823-7529
8676 N Crawford St., Portland, OR 97203
portlandoregon.gov/parks/finder/index.cfm?&propertyid=97&action=
ViewPark
In 1948, 15-year-old Thelma Taylor was kidnapped and murdered beneath the St.
Johns Bridge in Cathedral Park, and a walk in the park may bring you face-to-face
with her frightened ghost. To this day, Portland Police receive calls about a girl
screaming for help, but when they arrive they find no signs of trouble.

ComedySportz 503-236-8888
1963 NW Kearney St., Portland, OR 97209
portlandcomedy.com
Visitors go for the hilarious and talented comedy shows but may also be joined
by a laughing ghostly redhead who enjoys the shows as much as they do. Patrons

may also experience cold spots, lights switching off and on, and objects being moved right before their eyes.

Hours: Show dates and times vary, so please call the above number for more information.

Heathman Hotel 503-241-4100
1001 SW Broadway, Portland, OR 97205
portland.heathmanhotel.com

This 1927 hotel will pamper guests so much that many hate to leave, as with the ghosts of some former visitors. And anyone staying in rooms 703, 802, or 1003 may well have some unexpected roommates for the night. According to a prominent psychic, a suicide caused the hauntings when a guest jumped from room 1003, and all the rooms the jumping guest passed to his death are visited by his spirit.

Hollywood Theatre 503-281-4215
4122 NE Sandy Blvd., Portland, OR 97212
hollywoodtheatre.org

This 1921 theater is a wonderful place to catch either a movie or a live perfor-mance—but do not expect to watch it alone. Visitors should keep an eye out for the male ghost who seems to enjoy the upstairs lobby and the female ghost who is often seen relaxing in a seat in one of the back two rows.

Hours: Showtimes and event times vary, so please visit the website or call the above number for more information.

Lone Fir Pioneer Cemetery 503-797-1709
SE 26th Ave., Portland, OR 97214
oregonmetro.gov/historic-cemeteries/lone-fir-cemetery

Lone Fir Pioneer Cemetery is the oldest and probably most haunted cemetery in Portland. It is the resting place of both many famous Oregon pioneers and many infamous former Portland-area residents. Reports of shadows, glowing orbs, and even a screaming zombie-like ghost may make timid visitors want to think twice before venturing on the grounds after dark.

Oaks Park 503-233-5777
7805 SE Oaks Park Way, Portland, OR 97202
oakspark.com

This amusement park was built in 1890 and is the longest continually running amusement park in the nation. It is fun for the whole family, but be on the lookout for the ghost of a young girl in 1970s-style dress, especially near the merry-go-round, and for the young man who was killed in a fall from a trolley car.

Hours: March–September: Tuesday–Sunday, hours vary seasonally (typically noon–10 p.m. in the summer), so please visit the website calendar or call the above number for more information.

Shanghai Tunnels 503-622-4798
120 NW Third Ave., Portland, OR 97209
shanghaitunnels.info
The Shanghai Tunnels were an illegal underground labyrinth of tunnels that many were pushed into and taken through before being forced to work aboard ships as slave labor. Many who were drugged and pushed down into the tunnels died as a result of their injuries, and their ghosts may still wander the maze, seeking help and a way out.
　　Hours: Tour times and schedules vary, so please call the number listed above or visit the website for more information.

Stark Street
Portland, OR 97124
It is unusual for an entire neighborhood to be among the most haunted places in a city, but Stark Street in Portland is just that. Near many historic cemeteries and one-time flophouses, Stark Street was also the main thoroughfare for funeral processions and traveling to and from the Stark Street Ferry. People have captured a lot of paranormal happenings on camera and video here, and if you decide to take a midnight stroll along the street, you may not be alone.

White Eagle Tavern 503-282-6810
836 N Russell St., Portland, OR 97227
mcmenamins.com/452-white-eagle-home
Another location restored by Oregon's McMenamin brothers, White Eagle Tavern seems to be the residence of at least one ghost, who favors certain guest rooms on the second floor. Built in 1905, White Eagle's history has made the transition into the modern era, bringing its ghosts along with it.
　　Saloon hours: Monday–Thursday, 11 a.m.–1 a.m.; Friday, 11 a.m.–2:30 a.m.; Saturday, noon–2:30 a.m.; Sunday, 4 p.m.–11 p.m.
　　Hotel check-in: At the White Eagle Saloon, located on the first floor. Monday–Saturday, 4 p.m.–1 a.m.; Sunday, 4 p.m.–11 p.m.

Witch's Castle 503-823-2525
Forest Park, 4030–4040 NW Thurman St., Portland, OR 97229
portlandoregon.gov/parks/finder/index.cfm?action=
　　ViewPark&PropertyID=127

Follow the trails in Washington Park to find Witch's Castle. Stories of witchcraft, murder, and a family feud fuel the reports of ghostly sightings at this decrepit location.

Hours: Daily, 5 a.m.–10 p.m.

WILLAMETTE VALLEY

The Willamette Valley is the most heavily populated area in Oregon and is surrounded by towering mountain ranges to the east, west, and south. Much of its well-known fertility is the result of great Ice Age floods that swept soil down the Columbia River Gorge. During the 19th century, the area was mostly inhabited by the Kalapuya tribe of American Indians until as many as 90% of the tribe died from an epidemic of fever and ague between 1830 to 1833.

Bush House Museum 503-363-4714
600 Mission St. SE, Salem, OR 97302
salemart.org

The Bush House Museum is a 19th-century home that pays tribute to the wealthy Bush family and Oregon history. The home was loved so much by family members it is said that many of them have decided to spend the afterlife greeting visitors to the museum.

Bush House Tour hours: March 1–December 23: Wednesday–Sunday, 1, 2, 3, and 4 p.m.

Bush Barn Art Center hours: Tuesday–Friday, 10 a.m.–5 p.m.; Saturday–Sunday, noon–5 p.m.; closed on Monday.

Elsinore Theatre 503-375-3574
170 High St. SE, Salem, OR 97301
elsinoretheatre.com

While on a tour or watching a live performance or film at the Elsinore Theatre, visitors sometimes encounter the male ghost who is said to call out in the men's restroom, or the female ghost many have seen in the balcony area. Could it be that those who eagerly attended the grand opening in 1926 loved it so much that they never left?

Hours: Times for events, tours, and concerts vary, so please call the number above or visit the website for more information.

Oregon Coast

The Oregon coast runs along the edge of the Pacific Ocean and is defined to the east by the Oregon Coast Range of mountains. The coastline stretches about 260 miles, from the Columbia River at its north side to the California state line on the south. It is home to hundreds of species of wildlife, terrestrial and marine, including many birds, whales, and sharks. A pair of binoculars can keep a visitor occupied and amazed for hours on end.

Heceta Head Lighthouse 866-547-3696
92072 US 101 S., Yachats, OR 97498
hecetalighthouse.com
Built in 1892, Heceta Head Lighthouse is located exactly 13 miles from Florence and 13 miles from Yachats on scenic US 101. Its grounds are now a state park, the lightkeeper's house is an amazing bed-and-breakfast, and overall it is everything ghost stories are made of. The home of a frantic ghostly mother eternally seeking the burial place of her child, Heceta Head has been featured on nearly every paranormal show and documentary about America's most haunted locations. Chances are you will see or hear her if you stay here overnight.
Hours: Tour and event hours vary, so call the number above or visit the website for more information.

Marshfield Pioneer Cemetery 541-435-1177
700 Ingersoll Ave., Coos Bay, OR 97420
sites.google.com/site/cbcemetery
Marshfield Pioneer Cemetery was established in 1888 by the Independent Order of Odd Fellows. Age and landslides forced the relocation of many graves to a neighboring cemetery but many remain, some yet undiscovered. Perhaps the ghosts of those pleading to be found walk the grounds of the cemetery when the sun goes down. Pick up a key to the locked cemetery at the Coos Bay City Hall with a valid identification and a refundable $5 key deposit.

Old Wheeler Hotel 503-368-6000
495 US 101, Wheeler, OR 97147
oldwheelerhotel.com
Built in 1920, the Old Wheeler Hotel has been everything from an inn to a medical clinic to the vintage-style lodging it is today. There are many ghosts at Old

Wheeler, including women who chat in the hallways at night and a young boy who seems to enjoy the newfangled television sets. Will you be awakened during the night by one of these ghosts tugging on your blankets?

Office hours: 9 a.m.–8 p.m.

World War II Lookout Bunker 541-888-3778
Cape Arago Hwy., Charleston, OR 97420
oregonstateparks.org/index.cfm?do=parkPage.dsp_parkPage&parkId=66
On the pack trails of the Shore Acres State Park rests a piece of World War II history, a hollowed-out, roofless, four-room former lookout bunker. During the war, soldiers kept the coast safe by remaining vigilant for enemy ships. The rooms echo the past, and many have seen the ghost of a serviceman in uniform and recorded numerous electronic voice phenomena that corroborate its existence.

Hours: Daily, sunrise–sunset.

Directions: From US 101 in Coos Bay or North Bend, follow signs to Charleston and Ocean Beaches. Roads merge at a Y intersection in Coos Bay's Empire District, heading west on Newmark Avenue, which reaches the bay and turns left (south). The road, now Cape Arago Highway, continues 4 miles to Charleston. Continue on Cape Arago Highway heading south past Bastendorff County and Sunset Bay State Parks. A quarter mile south of Shore Acres, around a few turns, is the north end of the trailhead on the left (east) side of the road. The south end of the trailhead is located near the group picnicking area at Cape Arago State Park.

Yaquina Bay Lighthouse 541-265-5679
Newport, OR 97365
yaquinalights.org
The lighthouse was built in 1872, and the ghost stories began as early as 1899 with the publication of "The Haunted Lighthouse" by Lischen Miller in an issue of *Pacific Monthly.* It told the story of a young girl who was murdered at the lighthouse after being separated from her friends. Other accounts are of former light keepers who refuse to leave their posts. Take the guided tour and see what remnants of the past you bump into.

Tour hours: Thursday–Tuesday, noon–4 p.m. Sign up in the interpretive center. Tours are first come, first served, as space is limited.

SOUTHERN OREGON

Southern Oregon encompasses four counties—Douglas, Jackson, Klamath, and Josephine—west of the Cascade Mountain Range, not including the southern Oregon coast. Visitors will find many farms and ranches nestled among the many tree-covered hillsides and a population of nearly 500,000.

Darkwing Manor 541-512-1891
4192 Coleman Creek Rd., Medford, OR 97501
darkwingmanor.com
Darkwing Manor and Morguetorium Museum is located outside of Medford. It is an historic Gothic-style structure sitting back from the road among farms and ranches. The Morguetorium displays antique funerary items including mourning jewelry and attire, but it is the ghost of a little girl who loves to make her presence known that will grab your attention, even during the site's yearly award-winning Halloween attraction.
Tour hours: By appointment with four to five days advance notice. The cost is $5 per person with a four-person minimum.

Lithia Park 541-488-5340
340 S Pioneer St. (off Granite St. in upper Lithia Park), Ashland, OR 97520
ashland.or.us/Page.asp?NavID=14083
Lithia Park comprises 93 acres of forested canyon in Ashland. The scenery is a sight to behold with more than 90 acres of brilliantly green lawns, Japanese gardens, rose gardens, miles upon miles of wooded hiking trails, and beautiful groves of stately Sycamore trees. But also a sight to behold in a quite different way are the appearances of the park's ghosts, including those of a dog-faced boy and the young girl who was brutally raped and murdered in 1875 near the duck pond and now manifests over it as a mist.
Office hours: Monday–Friday, 8:30 a.m.–5 p.m.

Oregon Vortex 541-855-1543
4303 Sardine Creek L Fork Rd., Gold Hill, OR 97525
oregonvortex.com
Glimpse a strange world where the weird and unusual is commonplace, and challenge your mind to explain the visual and perceptual phenomena. While you are

at it, keep your eye out for the ghost of former landowner John Litster, who is said to lean against the crooked house and watch the tourists with a smile on his face.

Hours: March 1–October 31: Daily, 9 a.m.–5 p.m.

Schmidt House 541-479-7827
508 SW 5th St., Grants Pass, OR 97526
www.jocohistorical.org

A family home built by Claus Schmidt in 1901 is now an historic museum that highlights many of the family's personal belongings, furniture, and decor, and even clothing and a toy room. It is also said to still be the home of Schmidt sisters Anna and Flora.

Hours: Tuesday–Friday, 10 a.m.–4 p.m. Cost is $10 for the first person and $5 for each additional one in a group.

CENTRAL OREGON

Central Oregon is located in the middle of the state, with the Cascade Mountain Range that divides the state from north to south in the west, and the smaller Ochoco Mountain Range in the east that forms the western end of the Blue Mountain province. Part of an historically volcanic region, common sights include volcanic rock formations, lava beds, volcanic buttes, and crater lakes. Winter snowfalls also make central Oregon a great ski destination.

McCann House (also known as Congress House)
440 NW Congress St., Bend, OR 97701

Built between 1915 and 1916, this beautiful Georgian-style house is said to be cursed, and many tenants have died on the premises. Even more frightening are the flurry of brutal, unsolved murders just a stone's throw away from the home. The house is often part of the local historical society's Heritage Walks through historical Bend.

Hours: Contact the Deschutes County Historical Society at 541-389-1813 or visit deschuteshistory.org for more information on the Heritage Walks.

O'Kane Building
115 NW Oregon Ave., Bend, OR 97701
facebook.com/okanebuilding

The O'Kane Building has been continuously open since 1916 and has housed a theater, drugstore, apartments, offices, and many businesses that have long since disappeared. But even today local businesses and artists occupy the storefronts, inviting visitors to catch a glimpse of Bend history and maybe even get a peek of jovial original owner Hugh O'Kane. His ghost has been seen throughout the building, puffing on his cigar and leaving behind the lingering aroma of tobacco.
　　Hours: Daily, 7 a.m.–8:30 p.m.

Old St. Francis School 541-382-5174
700 NW Bond St., Bend, OR 97701
mcmenamins.com/421-old-st-francis-school-home
Another wonderful McMenamin brothers site, Old St. Francis School is right in the middle of downtown Bend. In 1936 it was a Catholic school, and today it contains a hotel, pub, brewery, bakery, restaurants, and a venue for live events. But be aware that you may awaken to find an unexpected guest looking at you from the foot of your bed, or you may hear ghostly children running and laughing in the on-site theater.
　　Old St. Francis Pub hours: Sunday–Thursday, 7 a.m.–11 p.m.; Friday–Saturday, 7 a.m.–1 a.m.
　　Fireside Bar hours: Monday–Thursday, 4 p.m.–1:30 a.m.; Friday, 3 p.m.–1:30 a.m.; Saturday–Sunday, noon–1:30 a.m.
　　O'Kane's hours: Monday–Thursday, 4 p.m.–11 p.m.; Friday, 4 p.m.–midnight; Saturday, 1 p.m.–midnight; Sunday, 1 p.m.–11 p.m.
　　More information: For theater hours, concerts, and events, call the number above or visit the website for more information.

Redmond Hotel
521 S Sixth St., Redmond, OR 97756
Built in 1927 by Alaskan pioneers William and Fanny Wilson, the Redmond Hotel was billed as the finest hotel east of the Cascade Mountains, and it remains one of the few intact examples of 20th-century Georgian architecture. In a paranormal vein, people have reported seeing a ghostly woman who likes to wander the halls and visit rooms of sleeping guests, hearing footsteps behind them when they are alone in rooms, and witnessing glowing orbs.

MOUNT HOOD–THE GORGE

Archeological digs have discovered that the Columbia River Gorge area has supported life for more than 13,000 years. The wide range of elevation makes this area even more curious, from 4,000 feet to sea level. With mountain trails and more than 90 waterfalls, this area attracts hikers, bicyclists, campers, fishermen, and those who love water sports and extreme winter sports.

Columbia Gorge Hotel 541-386-5566
4000 Westcliff Dr., Hood River, OR 97031
columbiagorgehotel.com
Built in 1921, the Columbia Gorge Hotel was dubbed the "Waldorf of the West" because numerous movie stars of the period, including Clara Bow and Rudolph Valentino, stayed in the elegant lodging. Just as glamorous today as it was in the roaring twenties, it has a few things now that it did not have then—the ghosts. It is said to be haunted by a bride who committed suicide after murdering her husband and a ghostly handyman who enjoys undoing what the living maintenance staff does. More than just a few people have hurriedly left during the night.

Edgefield 503-669-8610
2126 SW Halsey St., Troutdale, OR 97060
mcmenamins.com/54-edgefield-home
Another McMenamin location, Edgefield was originally a poor farm, housing those down on their luck. It later became a tuberculosis hospital, a home for troubled youth, and a nursing home. Today it is a hotel complete with restaurants, a theater, a golf course, an art gallery, and venues for live entertainment. Guests have seen a ghostly woman dressed in white, often accompanied by a child, and even a ghost dog that likes to push its nose under guests' bed covers. The front desk receives many calls from frightened guests who claim to hear children crying and screaming.
   Black Rabbit Restaurant and Bar hours: Daily, 7 a.m.–10 p.m.
   Power Station Pub hours: Sunday–Thursday, 11 a.m.–midnight;
   Friday–Saturday, 11 a.m.–1 a.m.
   Ruby's Spa and Salon hours: Sunday–Thursday, 9:30 a.m.–7 p.m.;
   Friday–Saturday, 8 a.m.–8 p.m.
   More information: For details about other on-site locations, call the number above or visit the website.

Eastern Oregon

Eastern Oregon includes the entire area east of the Cascade Mountain Range: Baker City, Bend, Burns, Hermiston, John Day, Klamath Falls, La Grande, Ontario, and the Dalles. Primary industries are timber, mining, and tourism. Those who enjoy the outdoors flock to the area to ski, hike, raft, and take in the local history.

Malheur Butte
US 20, about 7 miles east of Vale, OR 97918
Malheur Butte is an extinct volcano that is 15 million to 20 million years old. During its active period, it spewed lava that covered thousands of miles of land throughout Oregon, Washington, and northern California. With centuries-old tales of witch covens, imps, sprites, fairies, and ghosts, Malheur Butte has no shortage of paranormal activity.

Pioneer Park 541-276-8100
400 NW Despain Ave., Pendleton, OR 97801
pendletonparksandrec.com/parks_pioneer
The oldest park in the Pendleton area, Pioneer Park looks like any other children's playground at first glance. But if you look closer, among the playground equipment, you will see headstones protruding from the grass. People have witnessed mist-like figures, heard voices and footsteps behind them, and felt chilling cold spots on hot and humid days. Perhaps those whose graves have not yet been located are reaching out for help.
Hours: Daily, 5 a.m.–10 p.m.

Ye Olde Castle Restaurant 541-573-6601
186 W Monroe St., Burns, OR 97720
Ye Olde Castle Restaurant is an odd combination of 1950s-style home cooking and an antique museum that specializes in vintage bicycles and toys. If you love home-cooked meals and pies like Grandma used to make—and love the thought of catching a glimpse of the resident ghost, the Lady in Blue—Ye Olde Castle is the place to rest your bones, make your taste buds dance, and soothe your craving for ghosthunting all at the same time.
Hours: Breakfast, lunch, and dinner.

Additional Haunted Sites

BELOW I HAVE LISTED more than four-dozen haunted locations throughout the state of Oregon, beyond those given a detailed treatment elsewhere in this book. Some of these sites are also described in more depth at the *Ghosthunting Oregon* blog (**ghosthuntingoregon.blogspot.com**).

GREATER PORTLAND AREA

Buttertoes Restaurant 503-656-4383
5070 Linn Ln.
West Linn, OR 97068
Enjoy a meal and a visit with resident ghost Lydia, who seems to go out of her way to show herself to surprised diners at this eatery.

Columbian Cemetery 503-622-1615
1151 N Columbia Blvd.
Portland, OR 97211; savecolumbiancemetery.org
Visitors may encounter a sobbing female ghost who wanders the property, which was originally known as Love Cemetery.

Hayden Island 503-823 4524
12226 N Jantzen Dr.
Portland, OR 97217; myhaydenisland.com
Numerous ghosts, mostly laughing children, have been seen here, at what was formerly an early-20th-century amusement park and is now a shopping mall.

Hoodoo Antiques 503-360-3409
122 NW Couch St.
Portland, OR 97209; hoodooantiques.com
This shop is a wonderful place to admire antiques and perhaps experience one of the haunted objects, including a piano that plays itself and has inspired many police reports.

Kenilworth Park 503-823-7529
SE 34th Ave. and Holgate Blvd.
Portland, OR 97204; portlandoregon.gov/parks/finder/index.cfm?
    &propertyid=213&action=viewpark
During the day this park is a family destination, but at night it is the haunt of a young
girl who was raped and murdered and whose ghost is still calling out for help.

Lotus Nightclub 503-227-6185
932 SW Third Ave.
Portland, OR 97204; cegportland.com/lotus
Originally built in 1927, this fine-dining restaurant is also home to what many say
is a presence in the basement so evil that even employees refuse to talk about
their experiences there.

Old Town Pizza 503-222-9999
226 NW Davis St.
Portland, OR 97209; oldtownpizza.com
Old Town Pizza is situated above the Shanghai Tunnels, and its resident ghost,
Nina, makes frequent visits to the restaurant.

Pink Feather Restaurant 503-761-2030
14154 SE Division St.
Portland, OR 97233; facebook.com/thepinkfeather
It is said this restaurant was once a gathering place for underground gambling
and is still home to the ghosts of gamblers and prostitutes—and even a monkey
that would alert gamblers to police raids!

Pittock Mansion 503-823-3623
3229 NW Pittock Dr.
Portland, OR 97210; pittockmansion.org
Open to the public as a museum, this lavish home appears to remain occupied by
the spirits of the original owners, Henry and Georgiana Pittock.

Scaponia Recreation Site 503-397-2353
Scappoose-Vernonia Rd. (GPS: N45° 50.614' W123° 05.637')
Vernonia, OR 97056
co.columbia.or.us/departments/county-parks/scaponia
Approximately 15 miles north of Portland, this beautiful park is said to be haunted
by a man who was hanged as a horse thief by an angry mob.

Shilo Inn 503-297-2551
9900 SW Canyon Rd.
Beaverton, OR 97225; shiloinns.com
Guests at this hotel say it is not uncommon for them to hear disembodied footsteps and the voices of a spectral man and a woman while they rest for the night.

Tryon Creek State Park 503-636-4398
11321 SW Terwilliger Blvd.
Portland, OR 97219; tryonfriends.org
The sound of harnessed horses and men talking as they get ready for a workday
of cutting timber seems to precede oncoming storms at this site.

Villa St. Rose School for Girls
597 N Dekum St.
Portland, OR 97210
A former convent and Catholic girls school, this site is now on the Register of
Historic Places. The sound of girls running and laughing in the old gymnasium
is common.

WILLAMETTE VALLEY

Lee Mission Cemetery (D Street Cemetery) (Salem) 503-393-5461
D St. and Medical Center Dr.
Salem, OR 97308; leemissioncemetery.com
Keep an eye out for floating, mistlike apparitions when you pay your respects at
this historic cemetery that dates to the 19th century.

Mack Theater (McMinnville) 503-472-6225
510 NE Third St.
McMinnville, OR 97128; macktheater.com
While enjoying a movie at this theater that was built in 1941, visitors may experience unexplained cold spots and the overwhelming feeling of being watched,
especially in the ladies room.

Mission Mill (Salem) 503-585-7012
1313 Mill St. SE
Salem, OR 97301; willametteheritage.org

Once a thriving wool mill, this site is now a museum, where many have seen a young woman running across the bridge who is said to have been murdered on the property. Sometimes in the turbine room, people encounter the ghost of a man who lost his life maintaining machinery.

Old Pioneer Cemetery (Canby)
Knightsbridge Rd.
Canby, OR 97013
People have on many nights witnessed the ghost of an elderly gentleman wearing a suit and holding a leather pouch at this historic burial ground.

Oregon State Capitol (Salem)
900 Court St. NE
Salem, OR 97301; www.oregonlegislature.gov
Carpeting on the elevator floors of the state capitol building, which was twice destroyed by fire, will still sometimes mysteriously smolder with no known cause.

Pentacle Theatre (Salem) 503-364-7200
324 52nd Ave. NW
Salem, OR 97304; pentacletheatre.org
Live theater productions go hand in hand with the ghosts of actors from days gone by that are said to walk the aisles of the Pentacle Theatre.

Regal Albany Cinemas (Albany) 541-928-0069
1350 Waverly Dr. SE
Albany, OR 97322; regmovies.com
Enjoy a new-release film and perhaps catch a glimpse of the ghost dog that roams the aisles or the spectral lights that float across the stage.

Woodland Park Playground (Eugene) 888-267-2903
1699 N Terry St.
Eugene, OR 97402
The ghost of a young boy who was shot and killed at the park is said to warn visitors to leave before midnight.

OREGON COAST

Argonauta Inn Beach House (Cannon Beach) 503-436-2601
188 W Second St.
Cannon Beach, OR 97110
thewavescannonbeach.com/about/the-argonauta-inn
This inn is reported to be haunted by Ghengis Hansel, who disappeared into thin
air during a storm in 1952. Guests have seen wispy apparitions and felt a strong
and foreboding presence, especially near the inn's secret doors and passageways.

Egyptian Theatre (Coos Bay) 541-269-8650
229 S Broadway
Coos Bay, OR 97420; egyptiantheatreoregon.com
Enjoy classic films and live performances and possibly a ghost or two that likes to
make physical contact at this historic theater with an exotic flair.

Gracie's Sea Hag Restaurant and Lounge (Depoe Bay) 541-765-2734
58 US 101
Depoe Bay, OR 97341; theseahag.com
This eatery has been a favorite among tourists and locals alike in the years since it
opened in 1963. It's such a favorite that it seems many customers have remained
at the Sea Hag even after death has claimed them.

Liberty Theater (Astoria) 503-325-5922
1203 Commercial St.
Astoria, OR 97103; liberty-theater.org
Go for family entertainment and encounter the ghosts of murdered men in the
downstairs bathroom and another who was pushed from the balcony. The mirror
of the upstairs ladies room seems to display a female apparition.

Little Theatre on the Bay (North Bend) 541-756-4336
2100 Sherman Ave.
North Bend, OR 97459; ltob.net
Enjoy wonderful live performances and perhaps meet the presence in the projector room or the ghost of a young man who fell to his death from the catwalk.

Neahkahnie Mountain (Manzanita)

From Portland, drive west on US 26 about 70 miles to US 101, and then drive south on US 101 about 15.5 miles to the trailhead parking lot on the right. portlandhikersfieldguide.org/wiki/North_Neahkahnie_
Mountain_Trailhead

Enjoy the wondrous trails in this wilderness area, but be aware of the reports that many buried their African American slaves here and that their ghosts are said to walk the trails alongside the living.

Old City Hall (Coos Bay) 541-267-6507

375 Central Ave.

Coos Bay, OR 97420

Now offices and a nightclub, Old City Hall offers more than just liquid spirits, and visitors should listen for screams from the old jail cells and footsteps following them.

Seasider Hotel (Seaside) 503-717-1456

210 N Downing St.

Seaside, OR 97138

Once visited by John F. Kennedy during a trip to the Oregon coast, the Seasider is now home to mischievous ghosts that like to throw things across the rooms.

Tioga Hotel (Coos Bay)

275 N Broadway

Coos Bay, OR 97420

The Tioga Hotel is now apartments and businesses, but do not be surprised to see shadow figures darting about and to hear disembodied voices while you are in a room alone at this site.

Wildflower Grill (Lincoln City) 541-994-9663

4250 NE US 101

Lincoln City, OR 97367; wildflowergrill.blogspot.in

Enjoy a meal in the rustic restaurant, but do not be surprised if your bottom gets pinched by the playful ghost of Matilda.

SOUTHERN OREGON

Downtown Umpqua Bank (Roseburg) 541-440-3961

445 SE Main St.

Roseburg, OR 97470; umpquabank.com

This site is an active place once the lights go out, and people have encountered ghosts of a woman in 1920s attire and a man staring out the window. People have also heard others running up and down the stairs and seen papers flying across the room. The bottom elevator is almost always glowing red for no discernible reason, and nearly every night after the lights have been shut off, one on the top floor comes back on.

Herman Helms House (Jacksonville)

320 S Oregon St.

Jacksonville, OR 97530

Murder and suicide claimed the lives of a dozen family members in the 1800s, and the ghost of August Helms mourns the loss of her family still and can be heard crying throughout the house. The ghost of a little girl also sits on the stairs crying and is believed to be a Helms family member who died in 1868 of smallpox and is buried on the property.

Jacksonville Cemetery (Jacksonville) 541-899-1231

Cemetery Rd.

Jacksonville, OR 97530; friendsjvillecemetery.org

Strange green mists and a hooded figure are often reported at this historic cemetery that was dedicated in 1860.

Jacksonville Inn (Jacksonville) 541-899-1900

175 E California St.

Jacksonville, OR 97530; jacksonvilleinn.com

The oldest home in Oregon that now operates as an inn is also the haunt of an elderly female ghost seen walking the halls and interrupting diners in the bistro and wine room.

Justice Building (Medford) 541-774-4900

100 S Oakdale Ave.

Medford, OR 97501; courts.oregon.gov

Keep your eyes open on the fourth floor for lights switching on and off and doors slamming, and listen for the resident ghost calling out your name.

Linkville Pioneer Cemetery (Klamath Falls) 541-883-5351
Upham St. and East St.
Klamath Falls, OR 97601
ci.klamath-falls.or.us/your-government/city-dir/cemeteries
While paying your respects at this old municipal cemetery, look for strange moving lights and listen for disembodied voices whispering in your ear.

Linkville Playhouse (Klamath Falls) 541-884-6782
201 Main St.
Klamath Falls, OR 97601; linkvilleplayers.org
The ghost of an actor named Ralph is said to haunt this theater, playing music from the sound booth and sitting in the seats smoking a pipe while watching rehearsals. A light is now left on for him at night.

McCully House (Jacksonville) 541-899-2050
830 N Fifth St.
Jacksonville, OR 97530
countryhouseinnsjacksonville.com/mccullyhouseinn.jsp
Remember when you turn in for the night at this inn that the ghost of a woman in a long white gown may be roaming the hallways outside your door.

Rock Point Cemetery (Gold Hill)
Sams Valley Hwy.
Gold Hill, OR 97525
From I-5, take Exit 43, north of Gold Hill, and follow the signs to OR 99. Turn right on US 99, going toward Gold Hill. Go over the Rogue River, and the cemetery will be on the left. Visitors to this site have reported seeing a ghost that carries a lantern but that vanishes into thin air when they speak to him.

Wolf Creek Inn (Wolf Creek) 541-866-2474
100 Front St.
Wolf Creek, OR 97497; historicwolfcreekinn.com
Jack London completed his novel *The Valley of the Moon* here, and some say that his ghost remains in tribute to the happiest time of his life. A number of other reported ghosts are believed to be those of former owners and guests.

CENTRAL OREGON

Barlow Trail Roadhouse (Welches)
69580 US 26
Welches, OR 97067; barlowtrailroadhouse.com
There have been reports of televisions flying off their stands, glasses floating and falling, the sounds of bells ringing, and the overwhelming feeling of being watched and followed.

Lara House Lodge (Bend) 541-388-4064
640 NW Congress St.
Bend, OR 97701; larahouse.com
During a visit to this lovely, historic bed-and-breakfast, you may discover that you have a ghostly roommate that likes to move things in the night and whisper in your ear.

Pilot Butte Cemetery (Bend) 541-317-3000
Bear Creek Rd.
Bend, OR 97701; bend.or.us/index.aspx?page=746
Many people have reported seeing bright blue orbs that dance in the wind throughout this historic cemetery after dark.

Rhododendron Village (Rhododendron) 503-622-4798
73370 E Buggy Trail Dr.
Rhododendron, OR 97049; cgsstore.tripod.com/id25.html
This living history village, once a campsite used in the 1800s by pioneers on the Oregon Trail, was the site of many deaths. Today, volunteers report doors slamming shut and lights turning off and on, and unmarked graves are still being discovered on its grounds.

MOUNT HOOD—THE GORGE

Hood River Hotel (Hood River) 541-386-1900
102 Oak St.
Hood River, OR 97031; hoodriverhotel.com
It is said that the original owner haunts this hotel and accounts for disembodied footsteps, doors flying open and closed, and phone calls to the front desk from the elevator—while it is empty.

EASTERN OREGON

Candy Cane Park (La Grande) 541-962-1309
12th St. and J Ave.
La Grande, OR 97850
cityoflagrande.org/muraProjects/muraLAG/lagcity/index.cfm/
    city-facilities/parks/candy-cane-park
This site of an unsolved brutal hatchet murder in 1983 has been the subject of reports about the ghost of a young woman who enjoys the swings and can often be seen sitting quietly on park benches.

Geiser Grand Hotel (Baker City) 541-523-1889
1996 Main St.
Baker City, OR 97814; geisergrand.com
People report multiple ghosts at the Geiser, especially on the fourth floor, where a large happy party is heard loudly enough to warrant complaints from guests—but there is never actually a party happening on the floor. The Lady in Blue is seen walking up and down the hotel staircase, looking like a fashionable young woman from the 1920s.

Hot Lake Springs Hotel (La Grande) 541-963-4685
66172 OR 203
La Grande, OR 97850; hotlakesprings.com
Once an asylum and a nursing home, the resort is home to the ghost of a gardener who committed suicide on the grounds and who can sometimes be seen in the shadows with a spade in hand. The ghost of an old woman dislikes any changes made, and a young boy, whose right side is horribly disfigured, happily runs back and forth on the top floor.

Pendleton Arts Center (Pendleton) 541-278-9201
214 N Main St.
Pendleton, OR 97801; pendletonarts.org
Once a library, this site is said to be haunted by a librarian who committed suicide after a broken love affair and whose ghost can often be seen at night looking out of the darkened windows.

Ghostly Resources

THE FOLLOWING IS A LIST of resources to help road trippers and paranormal researchers map out their expeditions and learn more about ghosthunting in general.

America's Haunted Road Trip
americashauntedroadtrip.com; facebook.com/AHRT.books
Official website and Facebook page of the *America's Haunted Road Trip* series of travel guides, which feature haunted places that people can visit.

Reportedly Haunted Places in Oregon
wikipedia.org/wiki/reportedly_haunted_locations_in_Oregon
A detailed list of haunted locations in Oregon.

PSI of Oregon
psioforegon.com
Official site of author Donna Stewart's investigative team covers places it has visited.

Ghosthunting Oregon Blog
ghosthuntingoregon.blogspot.com
Supplemental material based on author Donna Stewart's personal visits to haunted places throughout the state.

Ghosthunting Oregon Facebook Page
facebook.com/ghosthuntingoregon
Continuously updated information about *Ghosthunting Oregon* and the subject matter it covers.

Portland Walking Tours: Beyond Bizarre Ghost Tours
portlandwalkingtours.com/tours/beyond-bizarre-ghost-tour
Information about haunted locations and tours in the Portland area.

Haunted Houses
hauntedhouses.com/states/or
A list of haunted locations throughout the state of Oregon.

Carpe Noctem
carpenoctem.tv/haunted-hotspots/oregon
A list of haunted locations in Oregon with descriptions of the hauntings.

Recommended Reading

THE FOLLOWING IS A LIST of a few books that I recommend to assist you in your ghosthunting adventures or to simply use as paranormal learning tools.

Danelek, J. Allan. *The Case for Ghosts: An Objective Look at the Paranormal.* Woodbury, MN: Llewellyn Publications, 2006.

Pari, Dustin, and Barry Fitzgerald. *The Complete Approach: The Scientific and Metaphysical Guide to the Paranormal.* Summer Wind Press, 2009.

Varhola, Michael, et al. *Ghosthunting Maryland.* Cincinnati, OH: Clerisy Press, 2010.

About the Author

DONNA STEWART is a paranormal researcher, radio host, writer, and founder of the Oregon 501(c)3 nonprofit Southern Oregon Project Hope. With a lifelong interest in the paranormal, she has devoted more than 30 years to research, mentoring new investigators, and cofounding the highly regarded paranormal research team Paranormal Studies and Investigations (PSI) of Oregon. She also hosts the long-running BlogTalkRadio show PSI-FI Radio. She is a native Oregonian and has called Coos Bay her home for most of her life.